Grandma's Recipes

igloobooks

igloobooks

Published in 2014
by Igloo Books Ltd
Cottage Farm
Sywell
Northants
NN6 0BJ
www.igloobooks.com

Food photography and recipe development: PhotoCuisine UK
Front and back cover images © PhotoCuisine UK

GUA006 0714
2 4 6 8 10 9 7 5 3 1
ISBN: 978-1-78343-477-0

Printed and manufactured in China

Contents

Breakfasts and Lunches

Strawberry compote with Greek yoghurt

SERVES: **4** | PREPARATION TIME: **5 MINUTES** | COOKING TIME: **10 MINUTES**

INGREDIENTS

250 g / 10 ½ oz / 1 ⅔ cups strawberries, chopped

2 tbsp caster (superfine) sugar

1 lemon, juiced

300 ml / 10 ½ fl. oz / 1 ¼ cups Greek yoghurt

PREPARATION METHOD

- Put the strawberries and sugar in a saucepan. Put a lid on the pan then cook over a gentle heat for 10 minutes, stirring occasionally.

- The compote is ready when there are no defined cubes of strawberry left in the mixture. Stir in the lemon juice and leave to cool completely.

- Spoon the compote into 4 dessert glasses and top with the yoghurt.

Pancakes with maple-poached apples

SERVES: **4** | PREPARATION TIME: **10 MINUTES** | COOKING TIME: **30 MINUTES**

INGREDIENTS

2 eating apples, peeled, cored and cut into wedges

250 ml / 9 fl. oz / 1 cup maple syrup

250 g / 9 oz / 1 ⅔ cups plain (all purpose) flour

2 tsp baking powder

2 large eggs

300 ml / 10 ½ fl. oz / 1 ¼ cups milk

2 tbsp butter

PREPARATION METHOD

- Put the apple in a small saucepan with the maple syrup and poach gently for 10 minutes or until the apples are soft all the way through.

- Mix the flour and baking powder in a bowl and make a well in the centre. Break in the eggs and pour in the milk then use a whisk to gradually incorporate all of the flour from round the outside. Melt the butter in a small frying pan then whisk it into the batter.

- Put the buttered frying pan back over a low heat. You will need a tablespoon of batter for each pancake and you should be able to cook 4 pancakes at a time in the frying pan.

- Spoon the batter into the pan and cook for 2 minutes or until small bubbles start to appear on the surface. Turn the pancakes over with a spatula and cook the other side until golden brown and cooked through.

- Repeat until all the batter has been used, keeping the finished batches warm in a low oven. Serve the pancakes with the apple slices spooned over the top.

Mini tuna omelette pizzas

SERVES: **4** | PREPARATION TIME: **5 MINUTES** | COOKING TIME: **8 MINUTES**

INGREDIENTS

4 large eggs, beaten

4 tbsp canned tomatoes, chopped

100 g / 3 ½ oz / ⅓ cup canned tuna, drained

1 mozzarella ball, diced

1 shallot, chopped

1 tbsp baby capers

PREPARATION METHOD

- Preheat the oven to 190°C (170°C fan) / 375F / gas 5 and oil a 4-hole Yorkshire pudding tin.
- Pour the beaten egg into the tin and bake in the oven for 4 minutes.
- Mix the tomatoes with the tuna, mozzarella, shallot and capers, then divide the mixture between the omelettes and return the tin to the oven for 4 minutes or until the edges are golden brown and the centre is set. Serve immediately.

Salmon and leek puffs

SERVES: **12** | PREPARATION TIME: **30 MINUTES** | COOKING TIME: **15 MINUTES**

INGREDIENTS

2 tbsp butter

2 leeks, sliced

450 g / 1 lb all-butter puff pastry

200 g / 7 oz salmon fillet, cut into 12 pieces

2 tbsp dill, chopped

1 egg, beaten

PREPARATION METHOD

- Heat the butter in a saucepan and fry the leeks for 10 minutes without colouring, then leave to cool completely.
- Preheat the oven to 200°C (180°C fan) / 400F / gas 6.
- Roll out half the pastry on a lightly floured surface and cut out 12 circles. Top each circle with a spoonful of leeks, a piece of salmon and a sprinkle of dill. Brush round the edges with beaten egg, then fold over the pastry and crimp the edges to seal.
- Score the tops lightly with a blunt knife, then brush with beaten egg.
- Bake the pastries for 15 minutes or until the underneaths are cooked through and the tops are golden brown.

Quiche Lorraine

SERVES: **6** | PREPARATION TIME: **1 HOUR** | COOKING TIME: **50 MINUTES**

INGREDIENTS

225 g / 8 oz / 1 ½ cups plain (all purpose) flour
110 g / 4 oz / ½ cup butter, cubed and chilled
200 g / 7 oz / 1 ⅓ cups smoked bacon lardons
2 tbsp olive oil
3 large eggs, beaten
225 ml / 8 fl. oz double cream
150 g / 5 ½ oz Gruyere, grated
mixed salad to serve
salt and pepper

PREPARATION METHOD

- Sieve the flour into a mixing bowl then rub in the butter until the mixture resembles fine breadcrumbs. Stir in just enough cold water to bring the pastry together into a pliable dough then chill for 30 minutes.
- Preheat the oven to 200°C (180°C fan) / 400F / gas 6.
- Roll out the pastry on a floured surface then use it to line a 24 cm (9 ½ in) loose-bottomed tart tin and prick it with a fork. Line the pastry with clingfilm and fill with baking beans or rice then bake for 10 minutes. Remove the cling film and beans and cook for another 8 minutes to crisp.
- Lower the oven to 150°C (130°C fan) / 300 F / gas 2. Fry the lardons in the oil for 5 minutes or until starting to brown.
- Whisk the eggs with the double cream until smoothly combined then stir in the lardons and half of the Gruyere. Season generously with salt and pepper.
- Pour the filling into the pastry case and scatter the rest of the cheese on top. Bake for 40 minutes or until just set in the centre. Leave the quiche to cool to room temperature, then cut into wedges and serve with a mixed salad

Beef empanadas

SERVES: **8** | PREPARATION TIME: **45 MINUTES** | COOKING TIME: **20 MINUTES**

INGREDIENTS

100 g / 3 ½ oz / ½ cup butter, cubed and chilled

200 g / 7 oz / 1 ⅓ cups plain (all purpose) flour

2 tbsp olive oil

1 onion, finely chopped

1 red pepper, diced

1 red chilli (chili), finely chopped

2 cloves of garlic, crushed

½ tsp Cayenne pepper

225 g / 8 oz / 1 cup minced beef

200 ml / 7 fl. oz / ¾ cup beef stock

1 egg, beaten

PREPARATION METHOD

- First make the pastry. Rub the butter into the flour until the mixture resembles fine breadcrumbs. Stir in just enough cold water to bring the pastry together into a pliable dough then chill for 30 minutes.

- Heat the oil in a large saucepan and fry the onion, pepper and chilli for 3 minutes, stirring occasionally. Add the garlic and Cayenne and cook for 2 minutes, then add the mince. Fry the mince until it starts to brown then add the stock and simmer for 20 minutes. Leave to cool completely.

- Preheat the oven to 200°C (180°C fan) / 400F / gas 6.

- Divide the pastry into 8 pieces and roll each piece out into a circle. Drain the filling of any excess liquid, then spoon it onto the pastry circles.

- Fold the pastries in half to enclose the filling then crimp round the edges to seal. Brush the pastries with the beaten egg.

- Bake the turnovers for 20 minutes or until the pastry is cooked through and crisp underneath.

Deep-fried tomato and mozzarella sandwiches

SERVES: **4** | PREPARATION TIME: **10 MINUTES** | COOKING TIME: **3–4 MINUTES**

INGREDIENTS

4 tbsp plain (all purpose) flour
1 egg, beaten
75 g / 2 ½ oz / ½ cup panko breadcrumbs
8 mozzarella slices
16 tomato slices
sunflower oil for deep-frying
rocket (arugula) leaves to serve

PREPARATION METHOD

- Put the flour, egg and panko breadcrumbs into 3 separate bowls.
- Sandwich each slice of mozzarella between 2 slices of tomato.
- Dip the tomato sandwiches alternately in the flour, egg and breadcrumbs and shake off any excess.
- Heat the oil in a deep fat fryer, according to the manufacturer's instructions, to a temperature of 180°C.
- Lower the tomato sandwiches in the fryer basket and cook for 3–4 minutes or until crisp and golden brown.
- Tip them into a kitchen paper lined bowl to remove any excess oil and serve immediately with some rocket on the side

Tomatoes stuffed with herb risotto

SERVES: **16** | PREPARATION TIME: **15 MINUTES** | COOKING TIME: **45 MINUTES**

INGREDIENTS

1 litre / 1 pint 15 fl. oz / 4 cups good quality vegetable stock

2 tbsp olive oil

1 onion, finely chopped

2 cloves of garlic, crushed

150 g / 5 ½ oz / ¾ cup risotto rice

50 g / 1 ¾ oz / ½ cup Parmesan, finely grated

2 tbsp butter

1 tbsp flat leaf parsley, chopped

1 tbsp chives, chopped

1 tbsp thyme leaves

16 large tomatoes

salt and pepper

PREPARATION METHOD

- Heat the stock in a saucepan, keeping it just below simmering point.
- Heat the olive oil in a sauté pan and gently fry the onion for 5 minutes without colouring. Add the garlic and cook for 2 more minutes then stir in the rice. When it is well coated with the oil, add 2 ladles of the hot stock. Cook, stirring occasionally, until most of the stock has been absorbed before adding the next 2 ladles. Continue in this way for around 15 minutes or until the rice is just tender.
- Preheat the oven to 190°C (170°C fan) / 375F / gas 5.
- Stir the Parmesan, butter and herbs into the risotto and season with salt and pepper. Cover the pan and take off the heat to rest for 4 minutes.
- Meanwhile, slice the tops off the tomatoes and scoop out the seeds. Arrange them in a baking dish. Beat the risotto really well, then season to taste with salt and pepper. Spoon the risotto into the tomato hollows, then replace the tops.
- Bake the tomatoes for 20 minutes or until tender.

Ham and dill pickle sandwich

MAKES: **2** | PREPARATION TIME: **5 MINUTES**

INGREDIENTS

4 slices granary bread
1 tbsp butter, softened
a handful of spinach leaves
8 wafer-thin slices smoked ham
75 g / 2 ½ oz / ⅓ cup crinkle-cut dill pickles
black pepper

PREPARATION METHOD

- Spread the bread with the butter then top 2 of the slices with spinach.
- Arrange the ham and pickles on top and season generously with black pepper.
- Lay the other slices of bread on top and serve straight away.

Chilli and garlic king prawns

SERVES: **2** | PREPARATION TIME: **5 MINUTES** | COOKING TIME: **5 MINUTES**

INGREDIENTS

2 slices crusty bread

3 tbsp olive oil

2 cloves of garlic, finely chopped

1 large mild red chilli (chili), finely chopped

12 raw king prawns, peeled with tails left intact

1 tbsp runny honey

½ lemon, juiced

1 tbsp flat leaf parsley, finely chopped

salad leaves to serve

PREPARATION METHOD

• Toast the bread in a griddle pan until nicely marked on both sides, then cut the slices in half and transfer to warm plates.

• Heat the oil in a frying pan, then fry the chilli and garlic for 2 minutes. Toss in the prawns, then stir-fry for 2 minutes or until they have turned opaque.

• Add the honey and lemon juice to the pan and toss well to coat, then divide the prawns between the two plates. Sprinkle with parsley and serve with salad leaves.

Saltimbocca with cherry tomatoes

SERVES: **4** | PREPARATION TIME: **15 MINUTES** | COOKING TIME: **8 MINUTES**

INGREDIENTS

4 veal escallops

4 large sprigs of rosemary

8 slices prosciutto

2 tbsp olive oil

12 cherry tomatoes, halved

2 tbsp balsamic vinegar

50 g / 1 ¾ oz / 2 cups baby spinach leaves

black pepper

PREPARATION METHOD

- Top each escallop with a sprig of rosemary and season with black pepper, then wrap them in prosciutto.
- Heat the oil in a large frying pan and fry the veal for 4 minutes on each side or until just cooked in the centre. Transfer to a warm plate and deglaze the pan with vinegar.
- While the veal is cooking, griddle the cut side of the cherry tomatoes.
- Serve the veal on a bed of spinach with the cherry tomatoes and pan juices spooned over.

Chicken, potato and pickled turnip salad

SERVES: **4** | PREPARATION TIME: **10 MINUTES** | COOKING TIME: **15 MINUTES**

INGREDIENTS

300 g / 10 ½ oz waxy salad potatoes, scrubbed and halved

150 g / 5 ½ oz / 1 cup cooked chicken, shredded

200 g / 7 oz / 1 ½ cups pickled turnips, drained

a few sprigs of flat leaf parsley

1 clove of garlic, crushed

1 small shallot, finely chopped

a pinch of caster (superfine) sugar

2 tbsp lemon juice

4 tbsp olive oil

salt and white pepper

PREPARATION METHOD

- Boil the potatoes in salted water for 15 minutes or until tender. Drain well, then toss with the chicken, turnips and parsley.

- Whisk together the garlic, shallot, sugar, lemon juice and oil and season to taste with salt and white pepper.

- Spoon the dressing over the salad, then serve warm straight away or chill for 1 hour and serve cold.

Starters

Fish soup

SERVES: **4** | PREPARATION TIME: **15 MINUTES** | COOKING TIME: **25 MINUTES**

INGREDIENTS

2 tbsp olive oil

1 onion, finely chopped

½ fennel bulb, finely chopped

3 cloves of garlic, crushed

2 tbsp tomato puree

2 tbsp Pernod

450 g / 1 lb small mixed whole fish

1 litre / 1 pint 15 fl. oz / 4 cups fish stock

croutons to serve

salt and pepper

PREPARATION METHOD

- Heat the oil in a saucepan and fry the onion and fennel for 10 minutes or until softened. Add the garlic and cook for 2 more minutes then stir in the tomato puree and Pernod.
- Add the fish to the pan then pour in the stock and bring to a simmer. Simmer for 20 minutes or until the fish are very soft.
- Transfer the contents of the pan to a liquidiser and blend until very smooth. Pass the soup through a sieve, then season to taste with salt and pepper.
- Serve with croutons.

Deep-fried Camembert with redcurrant jelly

SERVES: **4** | PREPARATION TIME: **10 MINUTES** | COOKING TIME: **4–5 MINUTES**

INGREDIENTS

4 tbsp redcurrant jelly
4 tbsp plain (all purpose) flour
1 egg, beaten
75 g / 2 ½ oz / ½ cup panko breadcrumbs
1 Camembert, cut into 8 wedges
sunflower oil for deep-frying
baby spinach leaves and chopped walnuts to serve

PREPARATION METHOD

- Put the redcurrant jelly, flour, egg and panko breadcrumbs in 3 separate bowls.
- Dip the Camembert wedges alternately in the jelly, flour, egg and breadcrumbs and shake off any excess.
- Heat the oil in a deep fat fryer, according to the manufacturer's instructions, to a temperature of 180°C.
- Lower the Camembert in the fryer basket and cook for 4–5 minutes or until crisp and golden brown.
- Tip the Camembert into a kitchen paper lined bowl to remove any excess oil and serve immediately.
- Serve with baby spinach leaves and chopped walnuts.

Meatballs in tomato sauce

SERVES: **6** | PREPARATION TIME: **30 MINUTES** | COOKING TIME: **30 MINUTES**

INGREDIENTS

4 tbsp olive oil

1 onion, finely chopped

1 clove of garlic, crushed

1 red chilli (chili), deseeded and finely chopped

250 g / 9 oz / 1 ⅔ cups minced veal

250 g / 9 oz / 1 ⅔ cups sausagemeat

50 g / 1 ¾ oz / ⅔ cup fresh white breadcrumbs

1 tsp dried oregano

1 egg yolk

1 sprig of rosemary

600 ml / 1 pint / 2 ½ cups tomato passata

salt and pepper

PREPARATION METHOD

- Heat half of the oil in a large sauté pan and fry the onion for 5 minutes or until softened.
- Add the garlic and chilli and cook for 2 more minutes, stirring constantly, then scrape the mixture into a mixing bowl and leave to cool.
- Add the mince, sausagemeat, breadcrumbs, oregano and egg yolk and mix well, then shape into golf ball-sized meatballs.
- Heat the rest of the oil in the sauté pan and sear the meatballs on all sides, then season with salt and pepper.
- Pour over the passata, then cover and simmer for 15 minutes or until the meatballs are cooked through.

Beer-battered onion rings

SERVES: **4** | PREPARATION TIME: **1 HOUR 45 MINUTES** | COOKING TIME: **25 MINUTES**

INGREDIENTS

1 large onion, peeled
300 ml / 10 ½ fl. oz / 1 ¼ cups milk
200 g / 7 oz / 1 ⅓ cups plain (all purpose)
2 tbsp olive oil
250 ml / 9 fl. oz / 1 cup pale ale
salt and pepper

PREPARATION METHOD

- Thickly slice the onion, then separate the slices into rings. Soak the onion rings in milk for 30 minutes, then drain well and pat dry with kitchen paper.

- Meanwhile, make the batter. Sieve the flour into a bowl then whisk in the oil and ale until smoothly combined. Season with salt and pepper.

- Heat the oil in a deep fat fryer, according to the manufacturer's instructions, to a temperature of 180°C.

- Dip the onion rings in the batter, then drop them straight into the hot oil. Fry for 3 minutes or until crisp and brown, then drain well and tip them into a kitchen paper lined bowl.

- Serve immediately.

Tomato and leek soup

SERVES: **4** | PREPARATION TIME: **15 MINUTES** | COOKING TIME: **40 MINUTES**

INGREDIENTS

2 tbsp olive oil

2 leeks, finely chopped

2 cloves of garlic, crushed

1 tbsp concentrated tomato puree

400 g / 14 oz / 2 cups ripe tomatoes, chopped

1 litre / 1 pint 15 fl. oz / 4 cups vegetable stock

2 tbsp flat leaf parsley, chopped

salt and pepper

PREPARATION METHOD

- Heat the oil in a large saucepan. Reserve 2 tbsp of the leek for a garnish and stir the rest into the oil with the garlic. Season with salt and pepper, then cook over a low heat for 10 minutes, stirring occasionally.

- Stir in the tomato puree, tomatoes and stock, then cover and simmer for 30 minutes.

- Transfer the soup to a liquidiser and blend until smooth, then pass the soup through a sieve to remove any seeds and bits of skin.

- Taste for seasoning then ladle the soup into warm bowls. Mix the reserved leek with the parsley and sprinkle on top.

Wiener schnitzel

SERVES: **4** | PREPARATION TIME: **15 MINUTES** | COOKING TIME: **4–5 MINUTES**

INGREDIENTS

4 tbsp plain (all purpose) flour

1 egg, beaten

75 g / 2 ½ oz / ½ cup panko breadcrumbs

4 veal escallops

sunflower oil for deep-frying

lemon wedges and parsley leaves to serve

PREPARATION METHOD

- Put the flour, egg and panko breadcrumbs in 3 separate bowls.
- Dip the escallops alternately in the flour, egg and breadcrumbs and shake off any excess.
- Heat the oil in a deep fat fryer, according to the manufacturer's instructions, to a temperature of 180°C.
- Lower the escallops in the fryer basket and cook for 4–5 minutes or until crisp and golden brown.
- Tip the schnitzel into a kitchen paper lined bowl to remove any excess oil, then serve immediately with lemon wedges and parsley.

Tomato soup

SERVES: **4** | PREPARATION TIME: **10 MINUTES** | COOKING TIME: **30 MINUTES**

INGREDIENTS

400 g / 14 oz / 2 cups ripe tomatoes

2 tbsp olive oil

1 onion, finely chopped

2 cloves of garlic, crushed

1 tbsp tomato puree

1 litre / 1 pint 15 fl. oz / 4 cups vegetable stock

4 tbsp double (heavy) cream

2 tbsp flat leaf parsley, chopped

salt and pepper

PREPARATION METHOD

- Score a cross in the top of the tomatoes and blanch them in boiling water for 30 seconds. Plunge them into cold water then peel off the skins. Cut the tomatoes in half and remove the seeds, then cut the flesh into small cubes.
- Heat the oil in a saucepan and fry the onion for 5 minutes or until softened. Add the garlic and cook for 2 more minutes then stir in the tomatoes and tomato puree. Pour in the vegetable stock and bring to the boil.
- Simmer for 20 minutes then blend until smooth with an emersion blender. Taste the soup and adjust the seasoning with salt and pepper.
- Ladle the soup into 4 warm bowls and stir a little cream into the top of each one. Garnish with parsley and grind over a little black pepper.

Tomato, mozzarella and sesame salad

SERVES: **2** | PREPARATION TIME: **5 MINUTES**

INGREDIENTS

2 large ripe tomatoes
1 mozzarella ball
½ tbsp balsamic vinegar
½ tbsp sesame oil
1 tsp sesame seeds
a handful of basil leaves
salt and pepper

PREPARATION METHOD

- Thickly slice the tomatoes and mozzarella and arrange them on 2 plates.
- Stir the vinegar and oil together and season with salt and pepper, then spoon it over the tomatoes and sprinkle with sesame seeds.
- Scatter over the basil leaves and serve immediately.

Winter minestrone

SERVES: **6** | PREPARATION TIME: **5 MINUTES** | COOKING TIME: **20 MINUTES**

INGREDIENTS

2 tbsp olive oil

1 onion, finely chopped

1 carrot, diced

1 celery stick, diced

1 tbsp rosemary, chopped

2 cloves of garlic, finely chopped

2 rashers streaky bacon, chopped

1.2 litres / 2 pints / 4 ¾ cups vegetable stock

150 g / 5 ½ oz / 1 ½ cups dried ditalini or similar pasta shapes

400 g / 14 oz / 2 cups canned tomatoes, chopped

3 tbsp Parmesan, grated

PREPARATION METHOD

- Heat the oil in a large saucepan and fry the onion, carrot and celery for 5 minutes without colouring. Add the rosemary, garlic and bacon and fry for 2 more minutes.
- Pour in the stock and bring to the boil, then add the pasta and cook for 10 minutes or until al dente.
- Stir in the canned tomatoes and return to the boil, then ladle into warm bowls and sprinkle with Parmesan.

Dinners

Cheese and chive quiche

SERVES: **6** | PREPARATION TIME: **1 HOUR** | COOKING TIME: **40 MINUTES**

INGREDIENTS

225 g / 8 oz / 1 ½ cups shortcrust pastry

3 large eggs, beaten

225 ml / 8 fl. oz double cream

3 tbsp chives, chopped

150 g / 5 ½ oz / 1 ½ cups smoked cheese, diced

150 g / 5 ½ oz / 1 ½ cups goats' cheese, diced

150 g / 5 ½ oz / 1 ½ cups Gruyère, grated

salt and pepper

PREPARATION METHOD

- Preheat the oven to 190°C (170°C fan) / 375 F / gas 5.

- Roll out the pastry on a floured surface and use it to line a 23 cm (9 in) round tart tin. Prick the pastry with a fork, line with cling film and fill with baking beans or rice.

- Bake the case for 10 minutes then remove the cling film and baking beans. Brush the inside with beaten egg and return to the oven for 8 minutes to crisp.

- Lower the oven to 150°C (130°C fan) / 300 F / gas 2

- Whisk the eggs with the double cream until smoothly combined then stir in the chives, smoked cheese, goats' cheese and half of the Gruyère. Season generously with salt and pepper.

- Pour the filling into the pastry case and scatter the rest of the Gruyère on top. Bake for 40 minutes or until just set in the centre.

Citrus-breaded bass fillets

SERVES: **4** | PREPARATION TIME: **15 MINUTES** | COOKING TIME: **4–5 MINUTES**

INGREDIENTS

75 g / 2 ½ oz / ½ cup panko breadcrumbs
1 lemon, zest finely pared
1 orange, zest finely grated
1 tbsp thyme leaves, finely chopped
4 tbsp plain (all purpose) flour
1 egg, beaten
4 sea bass fillets, skinned
sunflower oil for deep-frying
lemon wedges to serve

PREPARATION METHOD

- Mix the panko crumbs with the citrus zests and thyme leaves in a bowl, then put the flour and egg into 2 separate bowls.
- Dip the bass fillets alternately in the flour, egg and citrus breadcrumbs and shake off any excess.
- Heat the oil in a deep fat fryer, according to the manufacturer's instructions, to a temperature of 180°C.
- Lower the fish in the fryer basket and cook for 4–5 minutes or until crisp and golden brown.
- Tip the fish into a kitchen paper lined bowl to remove any excess oil, then serve immediately with lemon wedges.

Smoked haddock Raclette

SERVES: **6** | PREPARATION TIME: **15 MINUTES** | COOKING TIME: **15 MINUTES**

INGREDIENTS

450 g / 1 lb / 2–3 cups new potatoes, scrubbed and halved
1 head of broccoli, broken into florets
200 ml / 7 fl. oz / ¾ cup double (heavy) cream
2 tbsp horseradish sauce
400 g / 14 oz Raclette cheese, sliced
225 g / 8 oz smoked haddock, sliced

PREPARATION METHOD

- Boil the potatoes in salted water for 12 minutes or until tender, drain well.
- Meanwhile, blanch the broccoli in boiling salted water for 2 minutes, then refresh in iced water and drain well.
- Whip the cream with the horseradish sauce until it holds its shape, then spoon it into a serving bowl.
- Arrange the cheese, vegetables, smoked haddock and horseradish cream on a platter and set it in the middle of the dining table with a preheated Raclette grill. Each diner should fill one of the trays with a slice of cheese and their choice of vegetables and haddock before cooking it under the grill.

Mustard pork chops with peach chutney

SERVES: **4** | PREPARATION TIME: **15 MINUTES** | COOKING TIME: **10 MINUTES**

INGREDIENTS

4 pork chops

4 tbsp grain mustard

2 tbsp olive oil

1 onion, finely chopped

1 tsp fresh root ginger, finely chopped

1 red chilli (chili), finely chopped

2 peaches, peeled, stoned and diced

100 g / 3 ½ oz / ½ cup roasted red peppers in oil, drained and chopped

2 tbsp runny honey

2 tbsp rice wine vinegar

coriander (cilantro) to garnish

PREPARATION METHOD

- Preheat the grill to its highest setting.
- Spread the pork chops with mustard then grill for 3 minutes on each side or until just cooked in the centre. Leave to rest in a warm place for 5 minutes.
- Meanwhile, heat the oil in a saucepan and fry the onion, ginger and chilli for 5 minutes. Stir in the peaches, pepper, honey and vinegar then simmer for 5 minutes.
- Serve the chops with the warm chutney on the side and garnish with coriander.

Prosciutto-wrapped sausage sandwiches

SERVES: **2** | PREPARATION TIME: **5 MINUTES** | COOKING TIME: **15 MINUTES**

INGREDIENTS

4 pork and herb sausages

4 slices prosciutto

2 tbsp olive oil

2 bread rolls, halved

a handful of rocket (arugula) leaves

4 generous sprigs of sage (leaves separated)

PREPARATION METHOD

- Wrap the sausages with the prosciutto, then fry them in the oil over a low heat for 15 minutes, turning occasionally.
- Add the sage leaves to the frying pan for the last few minutes of cooking and remove when crisp.
- Meanwhile, toast the cut side of the rolls. When the sausages are ready, put them in the rolls with the rocket and sage leaves and serve immediately.

Barbecue baby back ribs

SERVES: **4** | PREPARATION TIME: **4 HOURS 30 MINUTES**

COOKING TIME: **3 HOURS 5 MINUTES**

INGREDIENTS

2 tbsp olive oil

1 small onion, grated

3 cloves of garlic, crushed

1 tbsp ginger, finely grated

1 tsp mixed spice

200 ml / 7 fl. oz / ¾ cup tomato passata

200 ml / 7 fl. oz / ¾ cup apple juice

3 tbsp dark brown sugar

1 ½ lemons, juiced

1 tbsp Worcester sauce

1 tbsp Dijon mustard

2 racks of baby back pork ribs, membrane removed

large pinch of salt

PREPARATION METHOD

- Heat the oil in a saucepan and fry the onion, garlic and ginger for 3 minutes without colouring. Stir in the mixed spice then add the passata, apple juice, sugar, lemon juice, Worcester sauce and mustard with a large pinch of salt and bring to the boil.

- Turn down the heat and simmer for 10 minutes or until the sauce is thick and smooth.

- Leave the sauce to cool, then brush half of it over the ribs and leave to marinate in the fridge for 4 hours or overnight.

- Preheat the oven to 110°C (90°C fan) / 225F / gas ¼.

- Transfer the ribs to a roasting tin and slow-roast for 3 hours, turning occasionally and basting with the rest of the sauce.

- The ribs can either be served straight away or cooked over a hot charcoal barbecue for a few minutes to give a smoky taste.

Pizza bianca with asparagus and tomatoes

MAKES: 1 | PREPARATION TIME: **2 HOURS 30 MINUTES** | COOKING TIME: **10–12 MINUTES**

INGREDIENTS

200 g / 7 oz / 1 ⅓ cups strong white bread flour, plus extra for dusting

½ tsp easy blend dried yeast

1 tsp caster (superfine) sugar

½ tsp fine sea salt

1 tbsp olive oil

2 tbsp crème fraiche

4 asparagus spears, halved lengthways

2 mushrooms, sliced

10 cherry tomatoes, halved

25 g / 1 oz / ¼ cup mozzarella cheese, grated

2 tsp thyme leaves

salt and pepper

PREPARATION METHOD

- Mix together the flour, yeast, sugar and salt and stir the oil into 140 ml / 5 fl. oz / ⅔ cup of warm water. Stir the liquid into the dry ingredients then knead on a lightly oiled surface for 10 minutes or until smooth and elastic.
- Leave the dough to rest covered with oiled cling film for 1–2 hours until doubled in size.
- Preheat the oven to 220°C (200 fan) / gas 7 and grease a non-stick baking tray.
- Knead the dough for 2 more minutes then roll it out into a big circle. Spread the base with crème fraiche, then arrange the asparagus, mushrooms and tomatoes on top. Scatter over the mozzarella and sprinkle with thyme, then season with a little salt and pepper.
- Bake the pizza for 10–12 minutes or until the base is cooked through underneath.

Chicken with couscous and broad bean salad

SERVES: **4** | PREPARATION TIME: **1 HOUR 10 MINUTES** | COOKING TIME: **15 MINUTES**

INGREDIENTS

2 limes, juiced

1 tbsp runny honey

4 chicken breast escallops

2 tbsp butter

salt and pepper

FOR THE COUSCOUS

150 g / 5 ½ oz / 1 cup baby broad beans, shelled

180 g / 6 oz / 1 cup couscous

1 shallot, finely chopped

1 tbsp mint leaves, finely chopped

1 lime, juiced

2 tbsp olive oil

PREPARATION METHOD

- Make a marinade for the chicken by mixing the lime juice and honey with a pinch of salt. Pour it over the chicken and marinate for 1 hour.
- Boil the broad beans in salted water for 6 minutes or until tender, plunge them into cold water to stop the cooking then drain well.
- Put the couscous in a bowl with a big pinch of salt and pour over 290 ml of boiling water. Cover the bowl tightly with cling film and leave to stand for 5 minutes.
- When the time is up, fluff up the grains with a fork and stir through the broad beans, shallot, mint, lime juice and oil. Season to taste with salt and pepper.
- Heat the butter in a large frying pan, then fry the chicken for 3 minutes on each side or until just cooked through. Serve with the couscous salad.

Mushroom, pea and leek filo pies

SERVES: **4** | PREPARATION TIME: **30 MINUTES** | COOKING TIME: **15 MINUTES**

INGREDIENTS

2 tbsp olive oil

1 large leek, chopped

2 cloves of garlic, crushed

250 g / 9 oz / 3 ⅓ cups button mushrooms, quartered

100 g / 3 ½ oz / ⅔ cup peas, defrosted if frozen

100 ml / 3 ½ fl. oz / ½ cup dry white wine

8 sheets filo pastry

50 g / 1 ¾ oz / ¼ cup butter, melted

salt and pepper

PREPARATION METHOD

- Heat the oil in a frying pan and fry the leek and garlic for 5 minutes without colouring. Add the mushrooms to the pan and season with salt and pepper, then cook for 10 minutes, stirring occasionally. Add the peas and wine and bubble until reduced by half. Season to taste with salt and pepper.
- Preheat the oven to 200°C (180°C fan) / 400F / gas 6.
- Divide the filling between 4 individual pie dishes. Brush the filo with melted butter, then scrunch up the sheets and lay them on top.
- Bake the pies for 15 minutes or until the pastry is crisp and golden brown.

Chicken with asparagus and rice noodles

SERVES: **2** | PREPARATION TIME: **1 HOUR 5 MINUTES** | COOKING TIME: **10 MINUTES**

INGREDIENTS

2 tbsp sesame oil

1 tsp Szechwan peppercorns, crushed

1 clove of garlic, crushed

1 tsp fresh root ginger, finely grated

2 skinless chicken breasts

10 asparagus spears, trimmed

2 tbsp vegetable oil

4 tbsp oyster sauce

3 spring onions (scallions), sliced diagonally

rice noodles to serve

PREPARATION METHOD

- Mix the sesame oil with the peppercorns, garlic and ginger and rub it into the chicken and asparagus. Leave to marinate for 1 hour.
- Heat the vegetable oil in a large frying pan and gently fry the chicken and asparagus for 8 minutes or until the chicken is cooked through, turning occasionally.
- Meanwhile cook the noodles according to the packet instructions, drain and keep warm.
- Stir 4 tbsp of water into the oyster sauce then add it to the pan. Bubble for 1 minute, turning the chicken and asparagus to coat.
- Sprinkle the spring onions over the chicken and serve with rice noodles.

Lamb chops with garlic and rosemary

SERVES: **4** | PREPARATION TIME: **5 MINUTES** | COOKING TIME: **10 MINUTES**

INGREDIENTS

2 tbsp olive oil

6 lamb chops, French-trimmed

2 cloves of garlic, thinly sliced

1 tbsp fresh rosemary

2 tbsp dry white wine

green beans to serve

salt and pepper

PREPARATION METHOD

- Heat the oil in a frying pan and season the lamb chops with plenty of salt and pepper. Fry the chops for 2 minutes on each side, then wrap them in a double layer of foil and rest for 5 minutes.
- Add the garlic and rosemary to the pan and stir-fry until the garlic just starts to turn golden, then remove from the pan and reserve.
- Add the wine to the pan to deglaze, then drizzle the pan juices over the lamb and sprinkle with the garlic and rosemary. Serve with green beans.

Sunshine chicken and vegetable stew

SERVES: **4** | PREPARATION TIME: **5 MINUTES** | COOKING TIME: **20 MINUTES**

INGREDIENTS

2 tbsp olive oil

450 g / 1 lb / 2 cups chicken breast, cubed

1 leek, sliced

1 celery stick, diced

2 cloves of garlic, crushed

400 g / 14 oz / 2 cups canned tomatoes, chopped

600 ml / 1 pint / 2 ½ cups chicken stock

1 lemon, juiced and zest finely grated

2 tbsp flat leaf parsley, chopped

salt and pepper

PREPARATION METHOD

- Heat the oil in a wide saucepan and sear the chicken pieces all over. Remove to a plate with a slotted spoon.
- Add the leek, celery and garlic to the pan and cook without colouring for 5 minutes. Pour in the tomatoes and stock and bring to the boil, then return the chicken to the pan and simmer gently for 10 minutes.
- Stir the lemon juice and zest into the stew and add salt and pepper to taste. Sprinkle over the parsley and serve immediately.

Grilled sea bream with fruit salad

SERVES: **4** | PREPARATION TIME: **25 MINUTES** | COOKING TIME: **4 MINUTES**

INGREDIENTS

½ tsp Chinese 5-spice

2 tbsp light soy sauce

4 sea bream fillets

200 g / 7 oz / 1 ½ cups sugar snap peas

1 cucumber

3 radishes, thinly sliced

1 tbsp sesame seeds

FOR THE FRUIT SALAD

2 small bananas, sliced

2 blood oranges, segmented

1 red chilli (chili), thinly sliced

2 tbsp coriander (cilantro) leaves

1 tbsp lime juice

½ tsp sesame oil

PREPARATION METHOD

- Stir the 5-spice into the soy sauce, then brush it over the bream fillets and leave to marinate for 10 minutes.
- Meanwhile, blanch the sugar snaps in boiling water for 3 minutes, then plunge into cold water and drain well. Peel the cucumber, then cut it in half lengthways and scrape out the seeds. Slice it thinly on the diagonal and toss it with the sugar snaps, radishes and sesame seeds.
- To make the fruit salad, combine all of the ingredients and divide between 4 small bowls.
- Preheat the grill to its highest setting. Grill the bream for 2 minutes on each side or until just cooked in the centre.
- Spoon the vegetables onto 4 plates and top with the bream fillets and serve the fruit salads on the side.

Chicken lasagne

SERVES: **6** | PREPARATION TIME: **30 MINUTES** | COOKING TIME: **30 MINUTES**

INGREDIENTS

2 tbsp olive oil

1 onion, finely chopped

2 cloves of garlic, crushed

300 g / 10 ½ oz / 2 cups chicken breast, diced

400 g / 14 oz / 2 ½ cups canned tomatoes, chopped

300 g / 10 ½ oz fresh lasagne sheets

3 mozzarella balls, thinly sliced

1 bay leaf

2 tbsp Parmesan, finely grated

salt and pepper

PREPARATION METHOD

- Heat the oil in a large saucepan and fry the onion for 3 minutes, stirring occasionally. Add the garlic and chicken and stir-fry for 5 minutes or until the chicken is nicely coloured. Pour in the tomatoes, then simmer for 10 minutes. Season to taste with salt and pepper.

- Preheat the oven to 190°C (170°C fan) / 375F / gas 5.

- Oil a large baking dish then layer up the lasagne sheets with the chicken mixture and mozzarella, finishing with a layer of mozzarella.

- Lay a bay leaf on top then sprinkle with Parmesan and bake for 30 minutes or until cooked through and golden brown.

Pappardelle with butternut and sage

SERVES: **4** | PREPARATION TIME: **5 MINUTES** | COOKING TIME: **15 MINUTES**

INGREDIENTS

400 g / 14 oz pappardelle

4 tbsp olive oil

½ butternut squash, peeled and thinly sliced

2 cloves of garlic, thinly sliced

½ tbsp thyme leaves

a small handful of sage leaves

1 lemon, juiced and zest finely grated

salt and pepper

PREPARATION METHOD

- Cook the pasta in boiling, salted water according to the packet instructions or until al dente.

- Meanwhile, heat the olive oil in a large frying pan and fry the squash for 8 minutes or until nicely browned, stirring occasionally. Add the garlic, thyme and sage to the pan and stir-fry for 2 more minutes, then stir in the lemon zest. Season to taste with salt and pepper.

- When the pasta is ready, reserve a ladleful of the cooking water and drain the rest. Tip the pasta into the butternut pan and toss well. If it seems too dry, add a little of the reserved cooking water and shake the pan to emulsify.

- Squeeze over a little lemon juice, then divide between 4 warm bowls and serve immediately.

T-bone steaks with garlic butter

SERVES: **2** | PREPARATION TIME: **5 MINUTES** | COOKING TIME: **15 MINUTES**

INGREDIENTS

sunflower oil for deep-frying

4 medium potatoes, cut into wedges

2 T-bone steaks

2 tbsp butter, softened

1 clove of garlic, crushed

1 tbsp flat leaf parsley, finely chopped

salad leaves to serve

salt and pepper

PREPARATION METHOD

- Preheat the grill to its highest setting and heat the oil in a deep fat fryer, according to the manufacturer's instructions, to a temperature of 130°C.
- Lower the potato wedges in the fryer basket and cook for 10 minutes so that they cook all the way through but don't brown.
- Pull up the fryer basket and increase the fryer temperature to 190°C. When the oil has come up to temperature, lower the fryer basket and cook the wedges for 5 minutes or until crisp and golden brown.
- While the wedges are cooking, season the steaks with salt and pepper and grill for 4 minutes on each side or until cooked to your liking. Leave to rest somewhere warm while you finish the wedges.
- Mix the butter with the garlic and parsley, then shape into 2 butter pats.
- Top each steak with a garlic butter pat and serve with the wedges and salad leaves.

Lentil burgers

SERVES: **4** | PREPARATION TIME: **30 MINUTES** | COOKING TIME: **35 MINUTES**

CHILLING TIME: **2 HOURS**

INGREDIENTS

250 g / 9 oz / 2 cups red lentils

2 spring onions (scallions), finely chopped

2 cloves of garlic, crushed

1 tsp ground cumin

1 tsp ground coriander (cilantro) seeds

100 g / 3 ½ oz / ⅔ cup gram flour

salt and pepper

TO SERVE

4 granary rolls, split

4 tbsp hummus

a handful of rocket (arugula)

1 courgette (zucchini)

1 carrot

2 spring onions (scallions), chopped

PREPARATION METHOD

- Cook the lentils in boiling water for 20 minutes or until tender, then drain well.
- Put the lentils in a food processor with the spring onions, garlic, spices and gram flour and pulse until evenly mixed. Season with salt and pepper.
- Shape the mixture into 4 burgers, then chill in the fridge for 2 hours.
- Preheat the oven to 200°C (180°C fan) / 400F / gas 6. Transfer the burgers to a greased baking tray and bake for 15 minutes or until cooked through.
- To build the burgers, spread the rolls with hummus and lay the burgers inside on a bed of rocket. Use a vegetable peeler to cut the courgette and carrot into ribbons and sprinkle over the spring onions. Season with salt and pepper and serve immediately.

Tagliatelle with prosciutto and tomatoes

SERVES: **4** | PREPARATION TIME: **5 MINUTES** | COOKING TIME: **12 MINUTES**

INGREDIENTS

400 g / 14 oz / 3-4 cups tagliatelle

6 slices prosciutto, chopped

100 g / 3 ½ oz / ⅔ cup cherry tomatoes, quartered

a handful of rocket (arugula)

a handful of basil leaves

4 tbsp extra virgin olive oil

PREPARATION METHOD

- Cook the tagliatelle in boiling, salted water according to the packet instructions or until al dente. Drain well.
- Return the pasta to the saucepan and toss with the rest of the ingredients, then divide between 4 warm plates and serve immediately.

Cod with stewed leeks and peppers

SERVES: **4** | PREPARATION TIME: **5 MINUTES** | COOKING TIME: **20 MINUTES**

INGREDIENTS

2 tbsp butter

3 leeks, sliced

175 ml / 6 fl. oz / ⅔ cup dry white wine

4 tbsp olive oil

4 portions cod fillet (skin on)

1 onion, sliced

3 red peppers, cubed

1 tsp smoked paprika

2 tsp caster (superfine) sugar

2 tbsp sherry vinegar

flat leaf parsley to garnish

PREPARATION METHOD

- Preheat the oven to 180°C (160°C fan) / 350F / gas 4.
- Heat the butter in an ovenproof frying pan then gently fry the leeks for 5 minutes without colouring. Turn up the heat and pour in the wine, then simmer for 2 minutes.
- Heat half of the oil in a separate frying pan and sear the skin-side of the cod portions. Transfer them to the top of the leeks, skin side up, then put the pan in the oven and roast for 10 minutes.
- Meanwhile, heat the rest of the oil in the cod pan and fry the onion and peppers for 8 minutes. Sprinkle over the paprika then stir in the sugar and vinegar and simmer for 2 minutes.
- Serve the cod on a bed of leeks with the peppers on the side. Garnish with parsley.

Tomato and salami tart

SERVES: **6** | PREPARATION TIME: **10 MINUTES** | COOKING TIME: **20 MINUTES**

INGREDIENTS

400 g / 14 oz / 1 large sheet ready-to-roll puff pastry

4 tbsp hummus

100 g / 3 ½ oz / ⅔ cup salami slices

3 medium tomatoes, sliced

4 black olives, pitted and sliced

a handful of rocket (arugula)

PREPARATION METHOD

- Preheat the oven to 220°C (200°C fan) / 425F / gas 7.
- Roll out the pastry into a rectangle on a lightly floured surface. Transfer the pastry to a non-stick baking tray.
- Spread the top of the pastry with hummus, leaving a 1 cm (½ in) border around the outside. Arrange the salami, tomatoes and olives on top.
- Transfer the baking tray to the oven and bake for 20 minutes or until the pastry is cooked through underneath. Scatter over the rocket and serve immediately.

Roasted root vegetables

SERVES: **4** | PREPARATION TIME: **45 MINUTES** | COOKING TIME: **45 MINUTES**

INGREDIENTS

200 g / 7 oz / 2 cups baby carrots, peeled

300 g / 10 ½ oz / 2 cups new potatoes, quartered

8 baby beetroot, halved

200 g / 7 oz / 2 cups shallots, peeled

1 bulb of garlic, broken into cloves

3 tbsp olive oil

salt and pepper

PREPARATION METHOD

- Preheat the oven to 190°C (170°C fan) / 375 F / gas 5.
- Tip the vegetables into a roasting tin and drizzle with the oil. Season well with salt and pepper, then roast for 45 minutes, stirring half way through.

Cotechino with borlotti beans

SERVES: **4** | PREPARATION TIME: **15 MINUTES** | COOKING TIME: **3 HOURS 30 MINUTES**

INGREDIENTS

1 cotechino sausage

1 onion, halved

1 carrot, cut into large chunks

1 celery stick, cut into large chunks

1 bouquet garni

300 g / 10 ½ oz / 2 cups freshly podded borlotti beans

2 tbsp olive oil

100 g / 3 ½ oz / ½ cup chargrilled peppers in oil, chopped

50 g / 1 ¾ oz / 2 cups rocket (arugula) leaves

50 g / 1 ¾ oz Pecorino

PREPARATION METHOD

- Put the cotechino in a large saucepan with the onion, carrot, celery and bouquet garni and pour over enough boiling water to cover by 5 cm (2 in). Simmer gently for 3 hours, then add the borlotti beans, topping up the water if necessary. Simmer for a further 20 minutes or until the beans are tender.

- Drain well and discard the carrot, onion, celery and herbs. Dry the outside of the cotechino with kitchen paper. Heat the oil in a frying pan and sear the cotechino until well browned on all sides.

- Toss the borlotti beans with the peppers and rocket and divide between four dishes. Cut the cotechino across into slices and arrange them on top, then use a vegetable peeler to shave over the Pecorino.

Tuna steak with tomato and caper salsa

SERVES: **2** | PREPARATION TIME: **10 MINUTES** | COOKING TIME: **6 MINUTES**

INGREDIENTS

2 tbsp olive oil

2 thick tuna steaks

salt and pepper

FOR THE SALSA

2 large ripe tomatoes

1 tbsp balsamic vinegar

3 tbsp extra virgin olive oil

1 tbsp capers

½ tbsp basil leaves, finely chopped

PREPARATION METHOD

- Score a cross in the top of the tomatoes and blanch them in boiling water for 30 seconds.
- Plunge them into cold water then peel off the skins.
- Cut the tomatoes in half and remove the seeds, then cut the flesh into small cubes.
- Whisk the balsamic vinegar into the oil, then stir in the tomatoes, capers and basil and season to taste with salt and pepper.
- Heat the oil in a large frying pan, then fry the tuna steaks for 3 minutes on each side or until golden brown, but still pink in the centre. Serve with the salsa spooned over.

Vegetable Raclette

SERVES: **6** | PREPARATION TIME: **5 MINUTES** | COOKING TIME: **2 MINUTES**

INGREDIENTS

1 head of broccoli, broken into florets
400 g / 14 oz / 1 ½ cups Raclette cheese, sliced
150 g / 5 ½ oz / 1 cup cherry tomatoes, quartered
75 g / 2 ½ oz / 1 cup button mushrooms, sliced

PREPARATION METHOD

- Blanche the broccoli in boiling salted water for 2 minutes, then refresh in iced water and drain well.
- Arrange the cheese and vegetables on a platter and set it in the middle of the dining table with a preheated Raclette grill. Each diner should fill one of the trays with a slice of cheese and their choice of vegetables before cooking it under the grill.

Rib-eye with tomatoes

SERVES: **1** | PREPARATION TIME: **10 MINUTES** | COOKING TIME: **6 MINUTES**

INGREDIENTS

1 large rib-eye steak
1 tbsp olive oil
1 sprig of rosemary
1 clove of garlic, halved
4 cherry tomatoes, halved
salt and pepper

PREPARATION METHOD

- Put a frying pan over a high heat and season the steak liberally with salt and pepper.
- Drizzle the oil over the base of the pan then lower in the steak and add the rosemary, garlic and tomatoes, cut side down, next to it.
- Cook without disturbing for 3 minutes, then turn everything over and cook for another 3 minutes. If you prefer your steak well-done, cook it for another 2–3 minutes on each side.
- Wrap the steak in a double layer of foil and leave to rest for 5 minutes, then serve with the tomatoes.

Turkey and vegetable pie

SERVES: **4** | PREPARATION TIME: **30 MINUTES** | COOKING TIME: **55 MINUTES**

INGREDIENTS

2 tbsp butter

1 onion, chopped

1 carrot, chopped

1 celery stick, chopped

1 tbsp plain (all purpose) flour

250 ml / 9 fl. oz / 1 cups milk

300 g / 10 ½ oz / 2 cups cooked turkey breast, cubed

150 ml / 5 ½ fl. oz / ⅔ cup crème fraiche

2 tbsp flat leaf parsley, finely chopped

450 g / 1 lb / 2 cups all-butter puff pastry

1 egg, beaten

PREPARATION METHOD

- Heat the butter in a saucepan and fry the onion, carrot and celery for 10 minutes without colouring. Sprinkle in the flour and stir well, then stir in the milk and bubble until it thickens. Add the turkey and crème fraiche and heat through, then season to taste with salt and white pepper. Stir in the parsley then leave to cool completely.

- Preheat the oven to 200°C (180°C fan) / 400F / gas 6.

- Roll out half the pastry on a lightly floured surface and use it to line a pie dish. Spoon in the filling and level the top, then brush round the rim with water. Roll out the rest of the pastry and lay it over the top then trim away any excess.

- Brush the top of the pie with beaten egg then bake for 45 minutes or until the pastry is cooked through underneath and golden brown on top.

Chicken, tomato and mushroom stew

SERVES: **4** | PREPARATION TIME: **5 MINUTES** | COOKING TIME: **30 MINUTES**

INGREDIENTS

2 tbsp olive oil

4 skinless chicken breasts, halved

1 onion, chopped

1 carrot, chopped

1 celery stick, chopped

2 cloves of garlic, crushed

400 g / 14 oz / 2 cups canned tomatoes, chopped

200 ml / 7 fl. oz / ¾ cup chicken stock

150 g / 5 ½ oz / 2 cups button mushrooms

mashed potato to serve

2 tbsp flat leaf parsley, finely chopped

salt and pepper

PREPARATION METHOD

- Heat the oil in a wide saucepan and sear the chicken all over. Remove to a plate with a slotted spoon.
- Add the onion, carrot, celery and garlic to the pan and cook without colouring for 5 minutes. Pour in the tomatoes and stock and bring to the boil, then return the chicken to the pan and simmer gently for 10 minutes.
- Add the mushrooms to the pan and simmer for another 10 minutes, then season to taste with salt and pepper.
- Serve the stew with mashed potato and the parsley sprinkled over.

Roasts

Poached chicken with creamy herb sauce

SERVES: **4** | PREPARATION TIME: **15 MINUTES** | COOKING TIME: **1 HOUR**

INGREDIENTS

1.5 kg / 3 lb 5 oz oven-ready chicken
4 shallots, sliced
a few sprigs of thyme
1 bulb of garlic, halved horizontally
1 lemon, halved
salt and pepper

FOR THE SAUCE

4 tbsp mayonnaise
4 tbsp double (heavy) cream
½ tsp Dijon mustard
1 tbsp flat leaf parsley, finely chopped
1 tsp thyme leaves, finely chopped
½ tbsp chives, finely chopped

PREPARATION METHOD

- Lay the chicken in a slow cooker and surround with the shallots, thyme, garlic and lemon. Pour over enough boiling water to cover the chicken by 2.5 cm (1 in), then simmer very gently for 20 minutes.
- Cover the pan, turn off the heat and leave the pan to cool to room temperature to complete the cooking.
- While the chicken is cooking, mix all of the sauce ingredients together and season to taste with salt and pepper.
- Joint the chicken and serve with the sauce spooned over.

Slow-roasted brisket with tomatoes

SERVES: **6–8** | PREPARATION TIME: **25 MINUTES** | COOKING TIME: **5 HOURS 30 MINUTES**

INGREDIENTS

2 tbsp butter

1 onion, finely chopped

2 cloves of garlic, crushed

75 g / 2 ½ oz / 1 cup fresh breadcrumbs

2 tbsp thyme leaves

2.5 kg / 5 ½ lb beef brisket

2 tbsp olive oil

6–8 small tomato vines

salt and pepper

PREPARATION METHOD

- Heat the butter in a frying pan and fry the onion and garlic with a big pinch of salt for 5 minutes or until softened, but not coloured. Take the pan off the heat and stir in the breadcrumbs and thyme. Leave to cool.

- Preheat the oven to 200°C (180°C fan) / 400F / gas 6. Unroll the beef brisket, then lay the stuffing in a line down the middle. Roll it back up and tie securely along the length with butchers' string.

- Rub the brisket all over with oil and season with salt and pepper, then transfer it to a shallow roasting tin and roast for 30 minutes.

- Reduce the oven to 140°C (120°C fan) / 275F / gas 1 and cover the brisket loosely with foil. Roast for 3 hours, basting every hour.

- Remove the foil and arrange the tomato vines around the outside of the beef, then return to the oven for 2 hours or until the beef is tender and the tomatoes are starting to collapse.

- Cover the roasting tin and leave to rest somewhere warm for 30 minutes before carving into thick slices.

Mediterranean chicken roulade

SERVES: **6** | PREPARATION TIME: **45 MINUTES** | COOKING TIME: **20 MINUTES**

INGREDIENTS

6 chicken breasts

450 g / 1 lb thin rindless pancetta rashers

225 g / 8 oz / 1 ⅓ cups soft goats' cheese

300 g / 10 ½ oz / 1 ½ cups chargrilled peppers in oil, drained

2 tbsp olive oil

mashed potato to serve

PREPARATION METHOD

- Lay the chicken breasts between two sheets of cling film and bash them flat with a rolling pin.
- Lay another sheet of cling film on the work surface and lay out the pancetta in a large rectangle with the rashers overlapping slightly. Arrange the chicken breasts on top in a single layer, then spread the with the goats' cheese. Arrange the peppers in a strip down the middle, then use the cling film to help you roll everything up into a tight cylinder. Twist the ends of the cling film to tighten the roll, then chill in the fridge for 30 minutes to set the shape.
- Unwrap the cling film, then tie along the length of the roulade with string. Put the roulade in a zip-lock bag and exclude as much air as possible before sealing. Bring a large pan of water to a simmer, then lower in the roulade, weighing it down with a trivet if necessary. Turn down the heat so that the water is barely bubbling and poach for 15 minutes.
- Carefully remove the roulade from the pan and discard the bag. Blot the surface dry with kitchen paper. Heat the oil in a large frying pan and sear the roulade all over to colour the pancetta. Cut into slices and serve with mashed potato.

Spice-crusted lamb salad

SERVES: **4** | PREPARATION TIME: **10 MINUTES** | COOKING TIME: **15 MINUTES**

INGREDIENTS

4 x 4-bone racks of lamb, French trimmed

3 tbsp tahini paste

2 tbsp ras el hanout spice mix

200 g / 7 oz / 1 cup canned chickpeas, drained

150 g / 5 ½ oz / 1 cup cherry tomatoes, quartered

½ cucumber, peeled, deseeded and chopped

150 g / 5 ½ oz / ⅔ cup feta, broken into chunks

2 handfuls of basil leaves

3 tbsp extra virgin olive oil

PREPARATION METHOD

- Preheat the oven to 220°C (200°C fan) / 425F / gas 7.
- Brush the lamb with tahini paste, then roll in the ras el hanout to coat. Transfer the racks to a roasting tin and roast in the oven for 15 minutes.
- Cover the lamb with a double layer of foil and leave to rest for 5 minutes.
- Toss the chickpeas, tomatoes, cucumber, feta and basil together and arrange on a large serving platter. Cut the lamb into 2-bone cutlets and position on top of the salad, then dress with olive oil.

Rosemary-roasted beef fillet

SERVES: **6** | PREPARATION TIME: **1 HOUR 20 MINUTES** | COOKING TIME: **35 MINUTES**

INGREDIENTS

6 tbsp olive oil

1 clove of garlic, finely chopped

3 tbsp rosemary, roughly chopped

1 kg / 2 lb 3 oz beef fillet

2 red peppers, cut into wedges

2 yellow pepper, cut into wedges

2 green peppers, cut into wedges

salt and pepper

PREPARATION METHOD

- Preheat the oven to 230°C (210°C fan) / 450F / gas 8.
- Mix of half the oil with the garlic and rosemary and season well with salt and pepper. Rub the mixture into the beef and leave to marinate for 1 hour.
- Transfer the beef to a roasting tin and roast for 35 minutes.
- Meanwhile, heat a griddle pan until smoking hot. Rub the rest of the oil into the peppers and season with salt and pepper. Griddle the peppers for 10 minutes or until nicely charred in places, turning occasionally.
- Move the beef to a warm plate, wrap with a double layer of foil and leave to rest for 10 minutes before carving into thick slices and serving with the peppers.

Pork chops with pesto

SERVES: **4** | PREPARATION TIME: **10 MINUTES** | COOKING TIME: **6 MINUTES**

INGREDIENTS

2 tbsp butter

4 pork chops, French-trimmed

2 tbsp balsamic vinegar

FOR THE PESTO

½ clove of garlic

1 ½ tbsp pine nuts, toasted

50 g / 1 ¾ oz / 2 cups basil leaves

25 g / 1 oz / ¼ cup Pecorino, finely grated

200 ml / 7 fl. oz / ¾ cup extra virgin olive oil

PREPARATION METHOD

- To make the pesto, crush the garlic with a pinch of salt in a large granite pestle and mortar until well pulped. Add the pine nuts and pound until broken up but not pasty. Add the basil a handful at a time and pound until well pulped then stir in the cheese and olive oil.

- Heat the butter in a shallowly ridged griddle pan. Fry the pork chops for 3 minutes on each side or until just cooked in the centre.

- Transfer the chops to 2 warm plates and stir the balsamic into the pan to deglaze. Drizzle the pan juices over the chops and serve with the pesto.

Minted lamb chops

SERVES: **4** | PREPARATION TIME: **2 HOURS** | COOKING TIME: **6 MINUTES**

INGREDIENTS

4 tbsp natural yoghurt, plus extra to serve

2 tbsp mint leaves, chopped

1 tsp Dijon mustard

1 lemon, zest finely grated

2 tbsp olive oil

8 lamb chops, French-trimmed

mint leaves and lemon wedges to serve

PREPARATION METHOD

- Mix the yoghurt with the mint, mustard, lemon zest and oil, then brush it over the lamb and leave to marinate for 2 hours.
- Preheat the grill to its highest setting.
- Grill the chops for 3 minutes on each side or until nicely browned, then serve garnished with mint leaves and lemon wedges.

Stuffed chicken legs with root vegetables

SERVES: **4** | PREPARATION TIME: **30 MINUTES** | COOKING TIME: **45 MINUTES**

INGREDIENTS

4 chicken thigh quarters

200 g / 7 oz / 1 ½ cup baby carrots, peeled

4 small parsnips, peeled and quartered

150 g / 5 ½ oz / 2 cups Jerusalem artichokes, peeled and halved

1 garlic bulb, halved horizontally

3 tbsp olive oil

salt and pepper

FOR THE STUFFING

2 tbsp butter

2 shallots, finely chopped

1 garlic clove, crushed

50 g / 1 ¾ oz / ⅔ cup fresh breadcrumbs

1 tbsp flat leaf parsley, finely chopped

2 cooking chorizo

PREPARATION METHOD

- First make the stuffing: heat the butter in a frying pan and fry the shallots and garlic for 4 minutes or until softened but not coloured. Take the pan off the heat and stir in the breadcrumbs and parsley. Skin the chorizo and crumble the meat into the stuffing, then mix well and season with salt and pepper. Leave to cool.

- Preheat the oven to 220°C (200°C fan) / 430 F / gas 7.

- Carefully slide your fingers between the skin and flesh of the thighs to create a pocket for the stuffing. Pack the stuffing inside the pocket and flatten it down with the palm of your hand. Close the ends with cocktail sticks.

- Mix the carrots, parsnips, Jerusalem artichokes and garlic together in a roasting tin and lay the chicken quarters on top. Drizzle with olive oil and season with salt and pepper.

- Transfer the tin to the oven and immediately reduce the temperature to 190°C (170°C fan) / 375 F / gas 5.

- Roast the chicken for 45 minutes or until the juices run clear when the thickest part is pierced with a skewer.

Italian roasted lamb rack

SERVES: **4** | PREPARATION TIME: **30 MINUTES** | COOKING TIME: **25 MINUTES**

INGREDIENTS

2 x 6-bone lamb racks, French-trimmed

salt and pepper

FOR THE STUFFING

1 tbsp olive oil

1 shallot, finely chopped

1 garlic clove, crushed

25 g / 1 oz / ⅔ cup fresh breadcrumbs

50 g / 1 ¾ oz / ½ cup pine nuts, roughly chopped

25 g / 1 oz / 1 cup basil leaves, roughly chopped

2 tbsp Parmesan, freshly grated

PREPARATION METHOD

- First make the stuffing: heat the oil in a frying pan and fry the shallot and garlic for 4 minutes or until softened but not coloured. Take the pan off the heat and stir in the rest of the ingredients, then season with salt and pepper. Leave to cool.
- Preheat the oven to 220°C (200°C fan) / 430 F / gas 7.
- Keeping a sharp boning knife parallel with the upper curve of the bones, slice into the meat to create a flap that can be opened out like a book. Do not cut all the way through.
- Divide the stuffing between the two racks, then fold the flaps back over and tie securely with butchers' string.
- Transfer the lamb to a roasting tin, then put it in the oven and immediately reduce the temperature to 190°C (170°C fan) / 375 F / gas 5.
- Roast the lamb for 25 minutes or until done to your liking. Transfer the rack to a warm serving plate, then cover with foil and leave to rest for 10 minutes before serving.

Roast chicken with carrots

SERVES: **4** | PREPARATION TIME: **10 MINUTES** | COOKING TIME: **1 HOUR 10 MINUTES**

INGREDIENTS

1.5 kg / 3 lb 5 oz chicken

3 tbsp olive oil

450 g / 1 lb / 2–3 cups small rainbow carrots, scrubbed

1 lemon, halved

1 tbsp flat leaf parsley, chopped

salt and pepper

PREPARATION METHOD

- Preheat the oven to 200°C (180°C fan) / 400F / gas 6.
- Season the chicken all over with sea salt and black pepper, then drizzle with olive oil and lay it breast side down in a large roasting tin.
- Transfer the tin to the oven and roast for 30 minutes.
- Turn the chicken breast side up and surround it with the carrots. Turn the carrots to coat them in the juices then roast for a further 40 minutes.
- To test if the chicken is cooked, insert a skewer into the thickest part of the thigh. If the juices run clear with no trace of blood, it is ready.
- Squeeze over the lemon halves and sprinkle with parsley before serving.

Duck breast with balsamic beetroot and watercress

SERVES: **4** | PREPARATION TIME: **15 MINUTES** | COOKING TIME: **1 HOUR**

INGREDIENTS

12 baby beetroot, stalks trimmed

4 duck breasts

2 tbsp balsamic glaze

50 ml / 1 ¾ fl. oz / ¼ cup port

150 ml / 5 ½ fl. oz / ⅔ cup duck stock

150 g / 5 ½ oz / 1 cup peas, defrosted if frozen

50 g / 1 ¾ oz / 3 cups watercress

roast potatoes to serve

PREPARATION METHOD

- Put the unpeeled beetroot in a saucepan of salted water and bring to the boil. Simmer for 30 minutes or until a skewer will slide easily into the centres. Plunge the beetroot into cold water, then slip off the skins.

- Preheat the oven to 200°C (180°C fan) / 400F / gas 6 and put a roasting tin in to heat.

- Lay the duck breasts skin side down in a single layer in a large frying pan. Put the pan over a medium heat and cook for 8 minutes, pouring off the fat into a jar when it gets too deep (the fat can be stored in the fridge and used for roasting potatoes). Transfer the duck breasts to the roasting tin in the oven, with the skin facing up and roast for 5 minutes.

- Meanwhile, add the balsamic and port to the frying pan and bubble for 1 minute then add the stock and boil for 3 minutes. Add the beetroot to the pan and warm through, stirring occasionally while the duck rests. Transfer the duck to a warm plate, cover with a double layer of foil and leave to rest for 10 minutes.

- Cook the peas in boiling salted water for 4 minutes, then drain well. Toss the peas with the beetroot and watercress and divide between 4 plates. Slice the duck breasts and transfer them to the plates, then spoon over the sauce. Serve with roast potatoes.

Desserts

Cranachan

SERVES: **4** | PREPARATION TIME: **15 MINUTES** | COOKING TIME: **5 MINUTES**

INGREDIENTS

1 tbsp butter

100 g / 3 ½ oz / 1 cup rolled porridge oats

4 tbsp runny honey

300 ml / 10 ½ fl. oz / 1 ¼ cups double (heavy) cream

3 tbsp Scotch whisky

200 g / 7 oz / 1 ⅓ cups raspberries

PREPARATION METHOD

- Heat the butter in a large frying pan then stir in the oats. Stir the oats over a medium heat for 3–4 minutes or until they turn golden. Stir in 2 tbsp of honey and cook until golden brown. Tip the oats into a bowl and leave to cool to room temperature.
- Whisk the cream with the whisky and the rest of the honey until softly whipped but not stiff. Lightly mash half of the raspberries and fold them into the cream.
- Divide the toasted oats between four dessert glasses and top with the raspberry cream.
- Spoon the rest of the raspberries on top and serve immediately.

Hazelnut profiteroles with pear sorbet

SERVES: **6** | PREPARATION TIME: **1 HOUR 15 MINUTES** | COOKING TIME: **20 MINUTES**

INGREDIENTS

55 g / 2 oz / ¼ cup butter, cubed

75 g / 2 ½ oz / ½ cup strong white bread flour, sieved

2 large eggs, beaten

3 tbsp hazelnuts (cobnuts), chopped

100 ml / 3 ½ fl. oz / ½ cup double (heavy) cream

1 tbsp Poire William liqueur

100 g / 3 ½ oz / ¾ cup dark chocolate (minimum 60 % cocoa solids), chopped

600 ml / 1 pint / 2 ½ cups pear sorbet

PREPARATION METHOD

- Preheat the oven to 200°C (180°C fan) / 400F / gas 6. Line a baking tray with greaseproof paper and spray with a little water.

- Melt the butter with 150 ml / 5 fl. oz / ⅔ cup water and bring to the boil. Immediately beat in the flour, off the heat, with a wooden spoon until it forms a smooth ball of pastry. Incorporate the egg a little at a time to make a glossy paste.

- Spoon the pastry into a piping bag fitted with a large plain nozzle and pipe 2.5 cm (1 in) buns onto the baking tray, then sprinkle with chopped hazelnuts.

- Bake for 20 minutes, increasing the temperature to 220°C (200°C fan) / 425F / gas 7 halfway through. Transfer the choux buns to a wire rack and make a hole in the underneath of each one so the steam can escape. Leave to cool completely.

- Heat the cream and liqueur to simmering point then pour it over the chocolate and stir to emulsify.

- Cut the choux buns in half and fill with sorbet, then serve 3 per person, drizzled with chocolate sauce.

Roasted peaches with marzipan

SERVES: **4** | PREPARATION TIME: **10 MINUTES** | COOKING TIME: **10 MINUTES**

INGREDIENTS

6 peaches, halved and stoned
100 g / 3 ½ oz / ⅓ cup marzipan
4 tbsp runny honey
2 sprigs of lavender

PREPARATION METHOD

- Preheat the oven to 180°C (160°C fan) / 355 F / gas 4.
- Arrange the peaches in a large baking dish and fill the stone cavities with marzipan. Roast for 10 minutes or until the peaches are soft to the point of a knife.
- Meanwhile, put the honey in a small pan with 4 tbsp of water and the lavender sprigs. Warm through for a few minutes to infuse.
- When the peaches are ready, divide them between 4 warm plates and pour any pan juices into the honey pan. Stir well, then spoon it over the peaches and serve.

Apple snow

SERVES: **6** | PREPARATION TIME: **15 MINUTES** | COOKING TIME: **20 MINUTES**

INGREDIENTS

2 large cooking apples, peeled and diced

3 tbsp light brown sugar

½ tsp ground cinnamon

FOR THE MERINGUE

4 large egg whites

110 g / 4 oz / ½ cup caster (superfine) sugar

2 tbsp flaked (slivered) almonds

PREPARATION METHOD

- Preheat the oven to 200°C (180°C fan) / 400F / gas 6.

- Put the apples, sugar and cinnamon in a saucepan with 4 tablespoons of cold water. Put a lid on the pan then cook over a gentle heat for 10 minutes, stirring occasionally. Taste the apple and stir in a little more sugar if it is too sharp.

- Whisk the egg whites until stiff, then gradually add the sugar and whisk until the mixture is thick and shiny.

- Spoon half of the apple compote into 6 ovenproof dessert glasses. Fold half of the meringue into the rest of the compote and spoon it on top, then add a final layer of meringue.

- Transfer the glasses to the oven and bake for 10 minutes or until the tops are golden brown.

Rum babas

SERVES: **12** | PREPARATION TIME: **1 HOUR 35 MINUTES** | COOKING TIME: **15–20 MINUTES**

INGREDIENTS

150 g / 5 oz / 1 cup plain (all purpose) flour

2 tsp dried easy-blend yeast

1 tbsp caster (superfine) sugar

½ tsp salt

3 large eggs, lightly beaten

75 g / 2 ½ oz / ⅓ cup butter, softened

300 ml / 10 ½ fl. oz / 1 ¼ cups double (heavy) cream

FOR THE SOAKING SYRUP

450 g / 1 lb / 2 cups caster (superfine) sugar

2 lemons, juiced

240 ml / 8 fl. oz / 1 cup rum

PREPARATION METHOD

- Oil a 12-hole silicone cupcake mould.

- Combine the flour, yeast, sugar and salt in a bowl and gradually whisk in half of the beaten egg with an electric whisk. Continuing to whisk, incorporate half of the butter, followed by the rest of the egg. Beat the remaining butter in with a wooden spoon, then divide the mixture between the moulds.

- Leave the babas to prove in a warm, draught-free place for 1 hour or until they have doubled in size. Preheat the oven to 200°C (180°C fan) / 400F / gas 6.

- Bake the babas for 10–15 minutes or until golden brown and cooked through, then turn them out onto a wire rack.

- Put the sugar in a saucepan with the lemon juice and 675 ml water and stir over a medium heat to dissolve the sugar. Boil the sugar water for 5 minutes or until it starts to turn syrupy, then stir in the rum. Transfer the babas to a mixing bowl, pour over the syrup and leave to soak until they've cooled completely.

- Whip the cream until it holds its shape, then spoon it into a piping bag fitted with a large star nozzle. Remove the babas from the syrup, then pipe a swirl of cream on top of each one.

Raspberry crème brûlée

SERVES: **4** | PREPARATION TIME: **45 MINUTES** | COOKING TIME: **5 MINUTES**

INGREDIENTS

450 ml / 12 ½ fl. oz / 1 ¼ cups whole milk

4 large egg yolks

75 g / 2 ½ oz / ⅓ cup caster (superfine) sugar

2 tsp cornflour (cornstarch)

1 tsp vanilla extract

2 tbsp raspberry jam (jelly), sieved

2 tbsp granulated sugar

PREPARATION METHOD

- Pour the milk into a saucepan and bring to simmering point.

- Meanwhile, whisk the egg yolks with the caster sugar, cornflour and vanilla extract until thick. Gradually incorporate the hot milk, whisking all the time, then scrape the mixture back into the saucepan.

- Stir the custard over a low heat until it thickens then divide it between 4 ramekins. Chill in the fridge for 25 minutes.

- Spread the raspberry jam over the top of the custards, then sprinkle with a thin even layer of granulated sugar. Caramelise the tops with a blowtorch and serve immediately.

Baked egg custard with peaches

SERVES: **4** | PREPARATION TIME: **20 MINUTES** | COOKING TIME: **50 MINUTES**

INGREDIENTS

1 x 420 g / 15 oz can peach slices in juice, drained

500 ml / 17 ½ fl. oz / 2 cups whole milk

2 large eggs, plus 1 egg white

50 g / 1 ¾ oz / ¼ cup caster (superfine) sugar

½ tsp vanilla extract

PREPARATION METHOD

- Preheat the oven to 160°C (140°C fan) / 325F / gas 3.

- Divide the peach slices between 4 ramekin dishes. Heat the milk in a saucepan until hot but not boiling.

- Meanwhile, stir the eggs, egg white and sugar together with the vanilla extract. When the milk is ready, incorporate it into the egg mixture in a thin stream, whisking all the time.

- Pass the mixture through a fine sieve and divide it between the ramekins. Set the ramekins in a large roasting in and pour enough boiling water around them to come half way up the sides.

- Transfer the tin to the oven and bake for 45 minutes or until the custards are just set in the centre and the tops are golden brown. Serve warm or chilled.

Millefeuille

SERVES: **4** | PREPARATION TIME: **30 MINUTES** | COOKING TIME: **30 MINUTES**

INGREDIENTS

450 g / 1 lb / 2 cups all-butter puff pastry

3 tbsp icing (confectioners') sugar

2 tbsp unsweetened cocoa powder

FOR THE CRÈME PATISSIERE

2 large egg yolks

50 g / 1 ¾ oz / ¼ cup caster (superfine) sugar

2 tbsp plain (all purpose) flour

2 tbsp cornflour (cornstarch)

1 tsp vanilla extract

225 ml / 8 fl. oz / ¾ cup whole milk

PREPARATION METHOD

- Preheat the oven to 220°C (200°C fan) / 425F / gas 7.

- Roll out the pastry on a lightly floured surface and cut it into 3 identical rectangles.

- Transfer the pastry to a baking tray and prick all over with a fork. Lay a second baking tray on top to weigh it down, then bake for 20 minutes or until the pastry is very crisp.

- Remove the top tray and dust the pastry heavily with icing sugar, then return to the oven for 5 minutes or until the sugar has caramelised. Leave to cool completely.

- To make the crème patissiere, stir the egg yolks, sugar, flours and vanilla extract together in a saucepan, then gradually add the milk.

- Heat the mixture until it starts to boil, stirring all the time, then take off the heat and beat vigorously to remove any lumps. Press a sheet of cling film onto the surface and leave to cool to room temperature.

- Sandwich the pastry sheets together with the crème patissiere and dust the top with cocoa, then cut into slices with a very sharp serrated knife.

Summer berry zabaglione

SERVES: **4** | PREPARATION TIME: **5 MINUTES** | COOKING TIME: **15 MINUTES**

INGREDIENTS

3 large egg yolks

2 ½ tbsp caster (superfine) sugar

2 ½ tbsp Marsala

4 sprigs of redcurrants

100 g / 3 ½ oz / ⅔ cup raspberries

100 g / 3 ½ oz / ⅔ cup blueberries

4 strawberries, sliced

PREPARATION METHOD

- Preheat the grill to its highest setting.
- Set a heatproof bowl over a saucepan of simmering water, making sure the bottom of the bowl doesn't come into contact with the water.
- Add the egg yolks, sugar and Marsala to the bowl and whisk vigorously until thick and creamy. Take the bowl off of the heat.
- Reserve one of the redcurrant sprigs for decoration and de-stem the rest. Mix them with the rest of the berries in a baking dish, then pour over the zabaglione.
- Top with the reserved redcurrant sprig, then toast the top under the grill for 2–3 minutes or until golden brown.

Almond and butterscotch semifreddo

SERVES: **6** | PREPARATION TIME: **1 HOUR** | COOKING TIME: **5 MINUTES**

FREEZING TIME: **6 HOURS**

INGREDIENTS

2 large eggs, separated

100 g / 3 ½ oz / 1 cup icing (confectioners') sugar

600 ml / 1 pint / 2 ½ cups double (heavy) cream

3 tbsp amaretto liqueur

50 g / 1 ¾ oz / ½ cup flaked (slivered) almonds

FOR THE BUTTERSCOTCH SAUCE

85 g / 3 oz / ½ cup butter

85 ml / 3 fl. oz / ⅓ cup double (heavy) cream

85 g / 3 oz / ¼ cup golden syrup

85 g / 3 oz / ½ cup dark brown sugar

PREPARATION METHOD

- Whisk the egg whites in a very clean bowl until stiff, then whisk in half of the icing sugar.
- Whisk the egg yolks with the rest of the icing sugar in a separate bowl for 4 minutes or until very thick.
- Whip the cream with the amaretto in a third bowl until it holds its shape. Fold the egg yolk mixture into the cream, then fold in the egg whites.
- Line a small loaf tin with cling film, then pour in the cream mixture and level the top. Freeze for 6 hours or preferably overnight.
- To make the butterscotch sauce, stir the butter, cream, syrup and sugar together over a low heat until the butter melts and the sugar dissolves. Increase the heat and simmer for 2 minutes or until thick and homogenised. Leave to cool to room temperature.
- Remove the semifreddo from the freezer 45 minutes before serving. Unmould it onto a serving plate and scatter over the almonds, then drizzle with the butterscotch sauce. Cut into 6 wedges and serve immediately.

Peach and ginger crumble

SERVES: **4** | PREPARATION TIME: **15 MINUTES** | COOKING TIME: **40 MINUTES**

INGREDIENTS

4 peaches, peeled, stoned and sliced
75 g / 2 ½ oz / ⅓ cup butter
50 g / 1 ¾ oz / ⅓ cup plain (all purpose) flour
25 g / 1 oz / ¼ cup ground almonds
2 tsp ground ginger
40 g / 1 ½ oz / ¼ cup light brown sugar

PREPARATION METHOD

* Preheat the oven to 180°C (160°C fan) / 350F / gas 4.
* Arrange the peaches in an even layer in a baking dish.
* Rub the butter into the flour and stir in the ground almonds, ground ginger and sugar. Take a handful of the topping and squeeze it into a clump, then crumble it over the fruit. Repeat with the rest of the crumble mixture then bake for 45 minutes or until the topping is golden brown.

Summer berry fool

SERVES: **6** | PREPARATION TIME: **15 MINUTES**

INGREDIENTS

300 ml / 10 ½ fl. oz / 1 ¼ cups double (heavy) cream

1 tsp vanilla extract

50 g / 1 ¾ oz / ½ cup icing (confectioners') sugar

300 ml / 10 ½ fl. oz / 1 ¼ cups thick Greek yoghurt

150 g / 5 ½ oz / 1 cup raspberries

150 g / 5 ½ oz / 1 cup blueberries

75 g / 2 ½ oz / ½ cup redcurrants

PREPARATION METHOD

- Whip the cream with the vanilla and icing sugar until it holds its shape, then fold in the Greek yoghurt.

- Reserve a few berries for decoration, then fold the rest in and divide the fool between 6 dessert glasses.

- Top with the rest of the berries and serve immediately.

Poached plums

SERVES: **4** | PREPARATION TIME: **5 MINUTES** | COOKING TIME: **10 MINUTES**

INGREDIENTS

8 plums

50 g / 1 ¾ oz / ¼ cup caster (superfine) sugar

250 ml / 9 fl. oz / 1 cup apple juice

1 orange, zest pared into ribbons

PREPARATION METHOD

- Put the plums in a saucepan with the sugar, apple juice and orange zest.
- Bring slowly to a simmer, then poach gently for 10 minutes or until the plums are tender to the point of a knife.
- Let the plums cool a little, then peel off and discard the skins. Serve warm or chilled.

Marinated strawberries with lemon sorbet

SERVES: **4** | PREPARATION TIME: **35 MINUTES**

INGREDIENTS

200 g / 7 oz / 1 ⅓ cups strawberries, sliced

2 tbsp balsamic vinegar

1 lemon, juiced

50 g / 1 ¾ oz / ¼ cup caster (superfine) sugar

4 small scoops lemon sorbet

PREPARATION METHOD

- Mix the strawberries with the vinegar, lemon juice and sugar and leave to marinate for 30 minutes.
- Divide the strawberries and their juices between 4 dessert glasses and top each one with a scoop of lemon sorbet.

Steamed fruit cake

SERVES: **8** | PREPARATION TIME: **OVERNIGHT** | COOKING TIME: **3 HOURS**

INGREDIENTS

350 g / 12 oz / 1 ¾ cups mixed dried fruit

55 ml / 2 fl. oz / ¼ cup brandy

110 g / 4 oz / ½ cup butter, softened

2 tbsp treacle

110 g / 4 oz / ½ cup dark brown sugar

2 large eggs, beaten

55 g / 2 oz / ⅓ cup self-raising flour

2 tsp mixed spice

1 tbsp ground almonds

pouring cream to serve

PREPARATION METHOD

- Mix the dried fruit with the brandy and leave to macerate overnight.
- Cream the butter, treacle and sugar together until well whipped then gradually whisk in the eggs, beating well after each addition. Sift over the flour and spice and fold in with the ground almonds and macerated dried fruit.
- Scrape the mixture into a large buttered pudding basin. Add a pleated sheet of buttered foil to the top and tie securely with string to make a handle.
- Steam the cake for 3 hours, making sure you check and top up the water if it starts to run low. Leave to stand for 10 minutes, then turn it out onto a plate and serve with cream.

Bakes

Gluten and dairy-free chocolate brownies

SERVES: **8** | PREPARATION TIME: **5 MINUTES** | COOKING TIME: **35 MINUTES**

INGREDIENTS

110 g / 4 oz dark chocolate (minimum 70% cocoa solids), chopped

85 g / 3 oz / ¾ cup unsweetened cocoa powder, sifted

225 g / 8 oz / 1 cup dairy-free baking spread

450 g / 1 lb / 2 ½ cups light brown sugar

4 large eggs

110 g / 4 oz / 1 cup rice flour

75 g / 2 ½ oz / ½ cup mixed nuts, chopped

PREPARATION METHOD

* Preheat the oven to 160°C (140°C fan) / 325F / gas 3 and oil and line a 20 cm x 20 cm (8 in x 8 in) square cake tin.
* Melt the chocolate, cocoa and baking spread together in a saucepan, then leave to cool a little.
* Whisk the sugar and eggs together with an electric whisk for 3 minutes or until very light and creamy.
* Pour in the chocolate mixture and sieve over the flour, then fold everything together with the nuts.
* Scrape the mixture into the tin and bake for 35 minutes or until the outside is set, but the centre is still quite soft.
* Leave the brownie to cool completely before serving.

Chocolate chip shortbread

SERVES: **16** | PREPARATION TIME: **20 MINUTES** | COOKING TIME: **15–20 MINUTES**

INGREDIENTS

225 g / 8 oz / 1 ½ cups plain (all purpose) flour
75 g / 2 ½ oz / ⅓ cup caster (superfine) sugar
150 g / 5 oz / ⅔ cup butter, cubed
50 g / 1 ¾ oz / ¼ cup chocolate chips

PREPARATION METHOD

- Preheat the oven to 180°C (160°C fan) / 355F / gas 4 and line a baking tray with greaseproof paper.
- Mix together the flour and caster sugar in a bowl, then rub in the butter. Knead gently with the chocolate chips until the mixture forms a smooth dough then divide it into 16 pieces.
- Roll each piece of dough into a ball, then flatten it onto the baking tray with the palm of your hand.
- Bake the biscuits for 15–20 minutes, turning the tray round halfway through. Transfer the biscuits to a wire rack and leave to cool.

Strawberry tarts

SERVES: **6** | PREPARATION TIME: **2 HOURS** | COOKING TIME: **15 MINUTES**

INGREDIENTS

225 g / 8 oz / 1 ½ cups plain (all-purpose) flour

110 g / 4 oz / ½ cup butter, cubed and chilled

FOR THE CRÈME PATISSIERE

2 large egg yolks

55 g / 2 oz / ¼ cup caster (superfine) sugar

2 tbsp plain (all purpose) flour

2 tbsp cornflour (cornstarch)

1 tsp vanilla extract

250 ml / 9 fl. oz / 1 cup milk

TO DECORATE

250 g / 9 oz / 1 ⅔ cups strawberries, quartered

icing (confectioners') sugar for dusting

mint leaves to garnish

PREPARATION METHOD

- Preheat the oven to 200°C (180°C fan) / 400F / gas 6.

- Sieve the flour into a mixing bowl then rub in the butter until the mixture resembles fine breadcrumbs. Stir in just enough cold water to bring the pastry together into a pliable dough.

- Roll out the pastry on a floured surface and cut out 6 circles then use them to line 6 tart tins. Line the tins with cling film and fill with baking beans then bake for 10 minutes. Remove the film and beans and return the cases to the oven for 2 minutes or until cooked through. Leave to cool.

- To make the crème patissiere, stir the egg yolks, sugar, flours and vanilla extract together in a saucepan, then gradually add the milk. Heat the mixture until it starts to boil, stirring all the time, then take off the heat and beat vigorously to remove any lumps. Spoon the crème patissiere into the tart cases and leave to cool.

- Pile the strawberries on top of the tarts and dust with icing sugar. Garnish with mint.

Apple, raspberry and marzipan puffs

MAKES: **20** | PREPARATION TIME: **20 MINUTES** | COOKING TIME: **15 MINUTES**

INGREDIENTS

400 g / 14 oz / 1 ¾ cups ready-to-roll puff pastry
150 g / 5 ½ oz / ½ cup marzipan, sliced
1 apple, cored and thinly sliced
300 g / 10 ½ oz / 2 cups raspberries
1 egg, beaten

PREPARATION METHOD

- Preheat the oven to 220°C (200°C fan) / 425F / gas 7.
- Roll out the pastry on a lightly floured surface, then cut out 20 circles with a fluted pastry cutter.
- Lay a slice of marzipan, a slice of apple and 3 raspberries on top of each one, then brush the edge with egg. Fold over the pastry circles to enclose the filling and press the edges firmly to seal.
- Transfer the pastries to a non-stick baking tray and bake for 15 minutes or until the pastry is cooked through.

Madeira cake with summer berries

SERVES: **8** | PREPARATION TIME: **10 MINUTES** | COOKING TIME: **55 MINUTES**

INGREDIENTS

200 g / 7 oz / 1 ⅓ cups self-raising flour, sifted
50 g / 1 ¾ oz / ½ cup ground almonds
175 g / 6 oz / ¾ cup caster (superfine) sugar
175 g / 6 oz / ¾ cup butter, softened
3 large eggs
1 lemon, zest finely grated
150 g / 5 ½ oz / 1 cup mixed summer berries
icing (confectioners') sugar for sprinkling

PREPARATION METHOD

- Preheat the oven to 160°C (140°C fan) / 325F / gas 3 and line a 23 cm (9 in) round cake tin with greaseproof paper.
- Combine the flour, ground almonds, sugar, butter, eggs and lemon zest in a bowl and whisk together for 2 minutes or until smooth.
- Scrape the mixture into the tin and level the top then bake for 55 minutes or until a skewer inserted into the centre comes out clean.
- Transfer to a wire rack and leave to cool completely. Pile the berries on top of the cake and dust lightly with icing sugar before serving.

Scones with yoghurt and jam

SERVES: **12** | PREPARATION TIME: **25 MINUTES** | COOKING TIME: **15 MINUTES**

INGREDIENTS

225 g / 8 oz / 1 ½ cups self-raising flour
55 g / 2 oz / ¼ cup butter
150 ml / 5 fl. oz / ⅔ cup milk
200 g / 7 oz / ¾ cup strawberry jam (jelly)
200 g / 7 oz / ¾ cup strawberry flavoured Greek yoghurt

PREPARATION METHOD

- Preheat the oven to 220°C (200°C fan) / 425F / gas 7 and oil a large baking sheet.

- Sieve the flour into a bowl and rub in the butter until the mixture resembles fine breadcrumbs. Stir in enough milk to bring the mixture together into a soft dough.

- Flatten the dough with your hands on a floured work surface until 2.5 cm (1 in) thick. Use a pastry cutter to cut out 12 circles and transfer them to the prepared baking sheet.

- Bake in the oven for 15 minutes or until golden brown and cooked through. Transfer the scones to a wire rack to cool completely

- Cut each scone in half and top with jam and yoghurt.

Meringues with strawberries and cream

SERVES: **4** | PREPARATION TIME: **30 MINUTES** | COOKING TIME: **1 HOUR**

INGREDIENTS

4 large egg whites
100 g / 3 ½ oz / ½ cup caster (superfine) sugar
1 tsp cornflour (cornstarch)
225 ml / 8 fl. oz / 1 cup double (heavy) cream
2 tbsp icing (confectioners') sugar
½ tsp vanilla extract
150 g / 5 ½ oz / 1 cup strawberries, quartered
mint leaves to garnish

PREPARATION METHOD

- Preheat the oven to 140°C (120°C fan) / 275F / gas 1 and oil and line a baking tray with greaseproof paper.
- Whisk the egg whites until stiff, then gradually whisk in half the sugar until the mixture is very shiny. Fold in the remaining sugar and the cornflour then spoon the mixture into four mounds on the baking tray.
- Bake the meringues for 1 hour or until crisp on the outside, but still a bit chewy in the middle. Turn off the oven and leave to cool completely inside.
- Whip the cream with the icing sugar and vanilla until it just holds its shape, then spoon it on top of the meringues. Scatter over the strawberries and garnish with mint leaves.

Cheese and bacon bread

MAKES: **1 LOAF** | PREPARATION TIME: **2 HOURS 30 MINUTES**

COOKING TIME: **35 MINUTES**

INGREDIENTS

400 g / 14 oz / 2 ⅔ cups strong white bread flour, plus extra for dusting

½ tsp easy blend dried yeast

1 tbsp caster (superfine) sugar

1 tsp fine sea salt

100 g / 3 ½ oz / 1 cup streaky bacon, chopped

100 g / 3 ½ oz / 1 cup Cheddar, grated

a small bunch of chives, chopped

PREPARATION METHOD

- Mix together the flour, yeast, sugar and salt. Stir the bacon, cheese and chives into 280 ml / 9 ½ fl. oz / 1 cup of warm water and stir into the dry ingredients.

- Knead the mixture on a lightly oiled surface for 10 minutes or until the dough is smooth and elastic. Leave the dough to rest in a lightly oiled bowl, covered with oiled cling film, for 1–2 hours or until doubled in size.

- Knead the dough for 2 more minutes then roll it into a fat sausage. Turn it 90° and roll it tightly the other way then tuck the ends under and transfer the dough to a lined baking tray, keeping the seam underneath. Cover the dough loosely with oiled cling film and leave to prove for 45 minutes.

- Preheat the oven to 220°C (200°C fan) / 430 F / gas 7.

- Transfer the tray to the top shelf of the oven. Bake for 35 minutes or until the underneath sounds hollow when tapped. Leave to cool completely on a wire rack before slicing.

Apricot and rosemary egg custards

SERVES: **4** | PREPARATION TIME: **30 MINUTES** | COOKING TIME: **45 MINUTES**

INGREDIENTS

500 ml / 17 ½ fl. oz / 2 cups whole milk

3 sprigs of rosemary

2 large eggs, plus 1 egg white

50 g / 1 ¾ oz / ¼ cup caster (superfine) sugar

4 tbsp apricot compote

PREPARATION METHOD

- Preheat the oven to 160°C (140°C fan) / 325F / gas 3.

- Heat the milk with the rosemary in a saucepan until hot but not boiling, then leave to infuse for 15 minutes.

- Meanwhile, stir the eggs, egg white and sugar together. When the milk is ready, incorporate it into the egg mixture in a thin stream, whisking all the time.

- Spoon the apricot compote into 4 ramekins, then pass the custard mixture through a fine sieve and divide it between them. Set the ramekins in a large roasting tin in and pour enough boiling water around them to come half way up the sides.

- Transfer the tin to the oven and bake for 45 minutes or until the custards are just set in the centre and the tops are golden brown. Serve warm or chilled.

Banana and cinnamon pastries

SERVES: **4** | PREPARATION TIME: **30 MINUTES** | COOKING TIME: **18 MINUTES**

INGREDIENTS

450 g / 1 lb / 2 cups puff pastry

100 g / 3 ½ oz / ½ cup dried banana chips

2 ripe bananas, peeled

3 tbsp light brown sugar

½ tsp cinnamon

1 egg, beaten

2 tbsp caster sugar

PREPARATION METHOD

- Preheat the oven to 220°C (200°C fan) / 430 F / gas 7.

- Roll the pastry out on a lightly floured surface and cut it into 4 squares.

- Put the banana chips in a plastic sandwich bag, then wrap the bag in a tea towel and crush with a rolling pin. Mash the bananas with a fork, then stir in the crushed banana chips, sugar and cinnamon.

- Spoon a quarter of the mixture in a line down the centre of each pastry square.

- Cut the exposed sides of the pastry into strips on the diagonal, then starting at the top, fold them across, alternating between the two sides as you work your way down.

- Transfer the pastries to a baking parchment-lined baking tray, brush with beaten egg and sprinkle with caster sugar.

- Bake the pastries for 18 minutes or until the pastry is puffy and golden on top and cooked through underneath. Serve warm or at room temperature.

Orange and caramel soufflés

SERVES: **4** | PREPARATION TIME: **45 MINUTES** | COOKING TIME: **12 MINUTES**

INGREDIENTS

1 orange

50 g / 1 ¾ oz / ¼ cup butter

3 tbsp caster (superfine) sugar

185 ml / 6 ½ fl. oz / ¾ cup whole milk

25 g / 1 oz / ⅙ cup plain (all purpose) flour

4 large eggs, separated

4 tbsp caramel syrup

PREPARATION METHOD

- Preheat the oven to 220°C (200°C fan) / 430 F / gas 8 and put a kettle of water on to boil.

- Finely grate the zest of the orange and set aside, then slice off the top and bottom. Slice away the peel then cut out each individual segment, leaving the white pith behind like the pages of a book. Discard the pith.

- Use half of the butter to grease four ovenproof tea cups then sprinkle the insides with a tablespoon of the sugar.

- Put the milk, remaining sugar and orange zest in a small saucepan and bring to simmering point. Meanwhile, melt the rest of the butter in a small saucepan. Stir in the flour then gradually incorporate the milk, stirring continuously to avoid any lumps forming. When the mixture starts to bubble, take the pan off the heat and beat in the egg yolks.

- Whip the egg whites with an electric whisk until they form stiff peaks. Stir a tablespoon of the egg white into the egg yolk mixture to loosen it then carefully fold in the rest of the egg white, retaining as much air as possible. Divide the mixture between the cups and level the tops with a palette knife. Run the tip of your thumb round the inside rim to create a lip as this will help the soufflés to rise evenly.

- Transfer the cups to a roasting tin and pour enough boiling water around them to come halfway up the sides. Bake for 12 minutes or until they are well risen and golden brown. Top with the orange segments and drizzle with caramel syrup, then serve immediately.

Shortbread rings

SERVES: **18** | PREPARATION TIME: **20 MINUTES** | COOKING TIME: **20 MINUTES**

INGREDIENTS

175 g / 6 oz / ¾ cup butter, softened

50 g / 1 ¾ oz / ¼ cup caster (superfine) sugar

½ tsp vanilla extract

175 g / 6 oz / 1 ¼ cups self-raising flour

1 egg, beaten

PREPARATION METHOD

- Preheat the oven to 170°C (150°C fan) / 340 F / gas 3 and line 2 baking trays with non-stick baking paper.

- Cream the butter, sugar and vanilla extract together with an electric whisk until pale and well whipped then stir in the flour.

- Spoon the mixture into a piping bag fitted with a large plain nozzle and rings of the mixture onto the trays.

- Brush the biscuits with egg, then bake for 20 minutes or until golden brown.

- Transfer the biscuits to a wire rack and leave to cool completely before serving.

Chocolate bundt cake

SERVES: **8** | PREPARATION TIME: **25 MINUTES** | COOKING TIME: **45 MINUTES**

INGREDIENTS

225 g / 8 oz / 1 cup butter, softened
225 g / 8 oz / 1 cup caster (superfine) sugar
4 large eggs, beaten
125 g/ 4 ½ oz / ¾ cup self-raising flour
100 g / 3 ½ oz / 1 cup ground almonds
3 tbsp unsweetened cocoa powder

TO FINISH

100 g / 3 ½ oz / ¾ cup dark chocolate (minimum 60 % cocoa solids), chopped
2 tbsp butter
2 tbsp golden syrup

PREPARATION METHOD

- Preheat the oven to 180°C (160°C fan) / 355F / gas 4 and butter a bundt tin.
- Cream the butter and sugar together until well whipped then gradually whisk in the eggs, beating well after each addition.
- Fold in the flour, ground almonds and cocoa then scrape the mixture into the tin.
- Bake the cake for 45 minutes or until a skewer inserted in the centre comes out clean. Turn the cake out onto a wire rack and leave to cool completely.
- Melt the chocolate, butter and syrup together over a low heat, stirring regularly, then spoon it over the cake.

Marmalade Breton gateau

SERVES: **6** | PREPARATION TIME: **15 MINUTES** | COOKING TIME: **40 MINUTES**

INGREDIENTS

250 g / 9 oz / 1 ¼ cups butter, cubed
250 g / 9 oz / 1 ¼ cups plain (all purpose) flour
250 g / 9 oz / 1 ¼ cups caster (superfine) sugar
5 large egg yolks
175 g / 6 oz / ½ cup marmalade
icing (confectioners') sugar for dusting
pinch of salt

PREPARATION METHOD

- Preheat the oven to 180°C (160°C fan) / 350F / gas 4 and butter a 20 cm (8 in) round loose-bottomed cake tin.
- Rub the butter into the flour with a pinch of salt then stir in the sugar. Beat the egg yolks and stir them into the dry ingredients. Bring the mixture together into a soft dough and divide it in two.
- Put 1 half on the freezer for 10 minutes. Press the other half into the bottom of the cake tin to form an even layer. Spread the marmalade on top. Coarsely grate the other half of the dough over the top and press down lightly.
- Bake the tart for 40 minutes or until golden brown and cooked through.
- Cool completely before unmoulding and dusting with icing sugar.

Lemon meringue pies

SERVES: **6** | PREPARATION TIME: **1 HOUR** | COOKING TIME: **30 MINUTES**

INGREDIENTS

100 g / 3 ½ oz / ½ cup butter, cubed

200 g / 7 oz / 1 ⅓ cups plain (all purpose) flour

225 g / 8 oz / 1 cup lemon curd

4 large egg whites

110g / 4 oz / ½ cup caster (superfine) sugar

PREPARATION METHOD

- Preheat the oven to 200°C (180°C fan) / 400F / gas 6.
- Rub the butter into the flour and add just enough cold water to bind. Chill for 30 minutes then roll out on a floured surface and cut out 6 circles with a large round cookie cutter. Use the pastry circles to line a 6-hole deep muffin tin and prick the bases with a fork.
- Line the pastry with cling film and fill with baking beans or rice then bake for 10 minutes. Remove the cling film and beans and cook for another 8 minutes to crisp. Fill the pastry cases with lemon curd.
- Whisk the egg whites until stiff, then gradually add the sugar and whisk until the mixture is thick and shiny. Spoon the meringue into a piping bag fitted with a large star nozzle and pipe a swirl on top of each pie. Return the tin to the oven to bake for 10 minutes or until golden brown. Serve hot or cold.

Snacks

Goats' cheese and pesto puffs

MAKES: **18** | PREPARATION TIME: **20 MINUTES** | COOKING TIME: **15 MINUTES**

INGREDIENTS

700 g / 1 ½ lb / 3 ½ cups all-butter puff pastry
100 ml / 3 ½ fl. oz / ½ cup pesto
150 g / 5 ½ oz / 1 cup white-rinded goats' cheese, cubed
1 egg, beaten

PREPARATION METHOD

- Preheat the oven to 220°C (200°C fan) / 430F / gas 7.
- Roll out the pastry on a lightly floured surface and cut it into 12 rectangles. Top each rectangle with a spoonful of pesto and a few cubes of goat's cheese, then brush round the edges with beaten egg.
- Fold the pastries in half and press the edges firmly to seal.
- Brush the pastries with beaten egg and bake for 15 minutes or until golden brown and cooked through.

Pepper and mozzarella turnovers

SERVES: **4** | PREPARATION TIME: **45 MINUTES** | COOKING TIME: **20 MINUTES**

INGREDIENTS

100 g / 3 ½ oz / ½ cup butter, cubed and chilled
200 g / 7 oz / 1 ⅓ cups plain (all purpose) flour
150 g / 5 ½ oz / ¾ cup chargrilled peppers in oil, drained
1 mozzarella ball, quartered
1 egg, beaten

PREPARATION METHOD

- First make the pastry. Rub the butter into the flour until the mixture resembles fine breadcrumbs. Stir in just enough cold water to bring the pastry together into a pliable dough then chill for 30 minutes.
- Preheat the oven to 200°C (180°C fan) / 400F / gas 6.
- Divide the pastry into 4 pieces and roll each piece out into a circle. Top with the peppers and mozzarella, then brush round the outside with egg.
- Fold the pastries in half to enclose the filling then crimp round the edges to seal.
- Bake the turnovers for 20 minutes or until the pastry is cooked through and crisp underneath.

Ham and cheese croquettes

SERVES: **6** | PREPARATION TIME: **25 MINUTES** | COOKING TIME: **4–5 MINUTES**

INGREDIENTS

4 tbsp plain (all purpose) flour
1 egg, beaten
75 g / 2 ½ oz / ½ cup panko breadcrumbs
450 g / 1 lb / 2 cups leftover mashed potato
100 g / 3 ½ oz / 1 cup Cheddar, grated
100 g / 3 ½ oz / ¾ cup cooked ham, finely chopped
sunflower oil for deep-frying
pinch of salt

FOR THE CARROT SALAD

2 tbsp lemon juice
2 tsp runny honey
3 carrots, grated

PREPARATION METHOD

- To make the carrot salad, mix the ingredients together with a pinch of salt and leave to marinate for 10 minutes.
- Put the flour, egg and panko breadcrumbs in 3 separate bowls.
- Mix the mashed potato with the cheese and ham then shape it into 12 parcels.
- Dip the croquettes alternately in the flour, egg and breadcrumbs and shake off any excess.
- Heat the oil in a deep fat fryer, according to the manufacturer's instructions, to a temperature of 180°C.
- Lower the croquettes in the fryer basket and cook for 4–5 minutes or until crisp and golden brown.
- Tip the croquettes into a kitchen paper lined bowl to remove any excess oil.
- Serve hot with the grated carrot salad on the side.

Individual cheese and onion quiches

MAKES: **6** | PREPARATION TIME: **30 MINUTES** | COOKING TIME: **35 MINUTES**

INGREDIENTS

225 g / 8 oz / 1 cup all-butter puff pastry

2 tbsp butter

1 large onion, quartered and sliced

3 large eggs, beaten

225 ml / 8 fl. oz / 1 cup double (heavy) cream

150 g / 5 ½ oz / 1 ½ cups Gruyère, grated

salt and pepper

PREPARATION METHOD

- Preheat the oven to 190°C (170°C fan) / 375 F / gas 5.
- Roll out the pastry on a floured surface and use it to line a 6-hole cupcake tin.
- Heat the butter in a frying pan and fry the onion for 10 minutes to soften.
- Whisk the eggs with the double cream until smoothly combined then stir in the onions and half of the Gruyère. Season generously with salt and pepper.
- Pour the filling into the pastry cases and scatter the rest of the Gruyère on top. Bake for 25 minutes or until the pastry is cooked through and the filling is just set in the centre.

Fried halloumi with Niçoise olives

SERVES: **2** | PREPARATION TIME: **10 MINUTES** | COOKING TIME: **2 MINUTES**

INGREDIENTS

2 tbsp olive oil

225 g / 8 oz / 1 block halloumi, sliced

FOR THE DRESSING

1 lemon, juiced

4 tbsp olive oil

½ clove of garlic, very thinly sliced

1 tbsp flat leaf parsley, finely chopped

1 tbsp coriander (cilantro) leaves, finely chopped

1 tbsp mint leaves, finely chopped

1 mild red chilli (chili), deseeded and finely chopped

50 g / 1 ¾ oz / ⅓ cup Niçoise olives

PREPARATION METHOD

- To make the dressing, whisk the lemon juice with the olive oil, then stir in the garlic, herbs, chilli and olives. Season with black pepper only, as the halloumi is quite salty.
- Heat the oil in a large frying pan and fry the halloumi slices for 1 minute on each side or until golden brown.
- Transfer to two warm plates and spoon over the dressing then serve immediately.

Mini Margherita pizza

SERVES: **6** | PREPARATION TIME: **2 HOURS 30 MINUTES** | COOKING TIME: **8 MINUTES**

INGREDIENTS

200 g / 7 oz / 1 ⅓ cups strong white bread flour, plus extra for dusting

½ tsp easy blend dried yeast

1 tsp caster (superfine) sugar

½ tsp fine sea salt

1 tbsp olive oil, plus extra for drizzling

3 tbsp tomato pizza sauce

150 g / 5 ½ oz mozzarella, grated

24 basil leaves

PREPARATION METHOD

- Mix together the flour, yeast, sugar and salt and stir the oil into 140 ml of warm water. Stir the liquid into the dry ingredients then knead on a lightly oiled surface for 10 minutes or until smooth and elastic.

- Leave the dough to rest covered with oiled cling film for 1–2 hours until doubled in size.

- Preheat the oven to 220°C (200°C fan) / 425F / gas 7 and grease a non-stick baking tray.

- Knead the dough for 2 more minutes then divide it into 6 equal pieces. Roll each piece of dough out into a circle, then spread it with pizza sauce and top with mozzarella. Arrange 4 basil leaves on top of each pizza, then drizzle with olive oil and sprinkle with salt and pepper.

- Bake the pizzas for 8 minutes or until the pizza dough is cooked through underneath.

Rose water meringues

SERVES: **16** | PREPARATION TIME: **20 MINUTES** | COOKING TIME: **1 HOUR**

INGREDIENTS

4 large egg whites

1 tbsp rose water

a few drops of pink food colouring

100 g / 3 ½ oz / ½ cup caster (superfine) sugar

PREPARATION METHOD

- Preheat the oven to 140°C (120°C fan) / 275F / gas 1 and oil and line a large baking tray with greaseproof paper.
- Whisk the egg whites until stiff with the rose water and food colouring, then gradually whisk in half the caster sugar until the mixture is very shiny. Fold in the remaining caster sugar with a large metal spoon, being careful to retain as much air as possible.
- Spoon the meringue into a piping bag fitted with a large plain nozzle and pipe 16 swirls onto the baking tray.
- Transfer the tray to the oven and bake for 1 hour. Turn off the oven and leave the meringues to cool slowly inside before serving.

Peanut millionaire's shortbread

MAKES: **6** | PREPARATION TIME: **20 MINUTES**

COOKING TIME: **3 HOURS 20 MINUTES** | CHILLING TIME: **2 HOURS**

INGREDIENTS

400 g / 14 oz can of condensed milk

150 g / 5 ½ oz / 1 cup salted peanuts

200 g / 7 oz dark chocolate (minimum 70% cocoa solids), chopped

50 g / 1 ¾ oz / ½ cup butter

FOR THE SHORTBREAD

225 g / 8 oz / 1 ½ cups plain (all purpose) flour

75 g / 2 ½ oz / ⅓ cup caster (superfine) sugar

150 g / 5 oz / ⅔ cup butter, cubed

PREPARATION METHOD

- Make the caramel layer in advance. Put the unopened can of condensed milk in a saucepan of water and simmer for 3 hours, adding more water as necessary to ensure it doesn't boil dry. Leave the can to cool completely.

- Preheat the oven to 180°C (160°C fan) / 350 F / gas 4 and line a 20 cm (8 in) square cake tin with greaseproof paper.

- To make the shortbread, mix together the flour and sugar in a bowl, then rub in the butter.

- Knead gently until the mixture forms a smooth dough then press it into the bottom of the tin in an even layer.

- Bake the shortbread for 20 minutes, turning the tray round halfway through. Leave to cool.

- Open the can of condensed milk and beat the caramel until smooth. Fold in the peanuts then spread it over the shortbread and chill for 1 hour.

- Put the chocolate and butter in a bowl set over a pan of simmering water and stir together until melted and smooth.

- Pour the mixture over the caramel layer and leave to cool and set before cutting into 6 bars.

Apricots with amaretti cream

SERVES: **4** | PREPARATION TIME: **2 HOURS 15 MINUTES** | COOKING TIME: **5 MINUTES**

INGREDIENTS

250 ml / 8 fl. oz / 1 cup unsweetened apple juice

300 g / 10 ½ oz / 1 ½ cups dried apricots

225 ml / 8 fl. oz / ¾ cup double (heavy) cream

2 tbsp icing (confectioners') sugar

2 tbsp amaretto liqueur

8 amaretti biscuits

PREPARATION METHOD

- Bring the apple juice to the boil, then pour it over the apricots and leave to cool and macerate for 2 hours.
- Whip the cream with the icing sugar and liqueur until it holds its shape, then spoon it over the apricots and crumble over the biscuits.

Index